Theorizing Tourism

Theorizing Tourism

Analyzing Iconic Destinations

Arthur Asa Berger

Left
Coast
Press
Inc.

Walnut Creek, California

2013

LEFT COAST PRESS, INC.
1630 North Main Street, #400
Walnut Creek, CA 94596
http://www.LCoastPress.com

ISBN 978-1-61132-234-7 hardcover
ISBN 978-1-61132-235-4 paperback
ISBN 978-1-61132-677-2 consumer eBook

Library of Congress Cataloging-in-Publication Data

Berger, Arthur Asa, 1933-
  Theorizing tourism : analyzing iconic destinations / Arthur Asa Berger.
    p. cm.
  Includes bibliographical references.
  ISBN 978-1-61132-234-7 (hardback : alk. paper) – ISBN 978-1-61132-235-4 (pbk. : alk. paper) – ISBN 978-1-61132-677-2 (consumer ebook)
  1. Tourism—Philosophy. 2. Tourism—Social aspects. I. Title.
  G155.A1B436 2013
  306.4'819—dc23
                                    2012034493

Printed in the United States of America

⊚™ The paper used in this publication meets the minimum requirements of American National Standard for Information Sciences—Permanence of Paper for Printed Library Materials, ANSI/NISO Z39.48–1992.

Left Coast Press, Inc. is committed to preserving ancient forests and natural resources. We elected to print this title on 30% post consumer recycled paper, processed chlorine free. As a result, for this printing, we have saved:

2 Trees (40' tall and 6-8" diameter)
1 Million BTUs of Total Energy
128 Pounds of Greenhouse Gases
697 Gallons of Wastewater
47 Pounds of Solid Waste

Left Coast Press, Inc. made this paper choice because our printer, Thomson-Shore, Inc., is a member of Green Press Initiative, a nonprofit program dedicated to supporting authors, publishers, and suppliers in their efforts to reduce their use of fiber obtained from endangered forests.

For more information, visit www.greenpressinitiative.org

Environmental impact estimates were made using the Environmental Defense Paper Calculator. For more information visit: www.papercalculator.org.

CONTENTS

Acknowledgments

Let me begin by expressing my appreciation to Mitch Allen, who suggested I write this book. Mitch and I have been meeting on Clement Street in San Francisco to have lunch for more than twenty years, and it was at one of our dim sum lunches that Mitch made his request. I had written a book on American iconic buildings and places for him earlier and the idea of a book on global iconic destinations and their place in the tourism industry made sense. I would like to thank Russell Johnson, president of Travel Media, for his photographs (of the Gaza Pyramids, the Great Wall of China, the Las Vegas Strip, and Masada), and his suggestions about the chapter on studying tourism, and Bob McKercher, a professor at the Hong Kong Polytechnic University School of Hotel and Tourism Management, for his comments about that chapter and for helping me get a number of photos of students at the school. I also want to thank Steve Goldberg for his photograph of the Eiffel Tower, Tuan Phong Li and Gloria Chan for their photos of the Potala Palace in Tibet, Gloria Chan for her photos of El Escorial and Bilbao, Spain, Ryan Harris for the photo of the Disneyland Castle, and Lynne Dearborn and John Stallmeyer for the photo of Luang Prabang, out of their book *Inconvenient Heritage*, also published by Left Coast. I took all the other photographs of tourist sites you will find in the book.

I became interested in writing about tourism thanks to the encouragement of Kaye Chon, dean of the School of Hotel and Tourism Management at Hong Kong Polytechnic University. I spent two months in Hong Kong at the school a few years ago, and I learned a great deal from talking about tourism and various other topics with my colleagues there, a very distinguished and highly productive group of tourism scholars. As you will see, I benefitted from the work of a large number of writers and scholars who have provided me with important ideas and insights into the fascinating topic of tourism. I have quoted a number of them so you can profit from their ideas.

[Travel] conveys the pleasure of learning new things and as Aristotle observed over 2,300 years ago, not only philosophers but people in general like learning things, even if the learning comes disguised as "entertainment." It is as learners that explorers, tourists, and genuine travelers, otherwise so different in motives and behavior, come together. Explorers learn the contours of undiscovered shorelines and mountains, tourists learn exchange rates and where to go in Paris for the best hamburgers....Travelers learn not just foreign customs and curious cuisines and unfamiliar beliefs and novel forms of government. They learn, if they are lucky, humility. Experiencing on their senses a world different from their own, they realize their provincialism and recognize their ignorance.... Why is travel so exciting? Partly because it triggers the thrill of escape, from the constriction of the daily, the job, the boss, the parents. "A great part of the pleasure of travel," says Freud, "lies in the fulfillment of...early wishes to escape the family and especially the father." The escape is also from the traveler's domestic identity, and among strangers a new sense of selfhood can be tried on, like a costume. The anthropologist Claude Lévi-Strauss notes that a traveler takes a journey not just in space and time (most travel being to places more ancient than the traveler's home) but "in the social hierarchy as well"; and he has noticed repeatedly that arriving in a new place, he has suddenly become rich (travelers to Mexico, China, or India will know the feeling). The traveler's escape, as least since the Industrial Age, has also been from the ugliness and racket of Western cities, and from factories, parking lots, boring turnpikes, and roadside squalor.

Paul Fussell, *The Norton Book of Travel*

I had read and frequently heard repeated, that of all methods of adorning the mind and forming judgment, travel was the most efficacious. I determined, therefore, on a plan of travelling, but to what part of the world to direct my course remained still to be chosen: I wished the scene of my observations to be new, or at least brilliant

Comte del Volney, eighteenth century traveler

Introduction

Tourism is now the largest industry in the world, employing millions of people in a variety of occupations related to travel. Graduates of tourism programs in universities work in government agencies, travel agencies, hotels, museums, sports venues, medical facilities, and universities, and have positions such as hotel managers, marketing directors, travel agents, travel writers, and professors of tourism studies. Given the size and importance of the tourism industry, it is only logical that many universities now offer courses on tourism and majors in tourism studies to fill the demands of the tourism industry for people with knowledge and expertise in the field. This book is designed both for tourists and for tourism students and deals with the subject by focusing on the iconic places and buildings tourists visit—on their their social, cultural, semiotic, and economic significance.

To frame the book, the first chapter deals with ways we study tourism. Since there are many different kinds of tourism, such as cultural tourism, sexual tourism, adventure tourism, eco-tourism, medical tourism, sports tourism, and disaster tourism, there is a need to explain how tourism, in general, might be studied. So the chapter deals with topics such as typologies about the kinds of tourists that exist and their motivations, as well as theories and controversies in the field of tourism research. Tourism scholars do research on such diverse topics as the way tourists use the internet, forecasting tourist demand, marketing to tourists, various theories about the nature of tourism, and applied aspects of tourism such as hotel management. My chapter on the study of tourism focuses upon important theories about the nature of tourism and upon how tourism can be studied. I also deal with other theories and concepts related to tourism and apply them in later chapters.

The second chapter deals with the semiotic analysis of tourism, since that science focuses upon the fact that all the iconic buildings and places I discuss can be seen as signs, a sign being anything that can be used to stand for something else or anything that generates information about something. Our hair color, hair styles, facial expressions and body language are all signs that reveal things about us. So are words and objects; for some semioticians, just about everything is a sign. Semiotics, the science of signs, is the core methodology, I would suggest, of cultural studies—an interdisciplinary approach that uses semiotics, psychoanalytic theory, sociological theory, Marxist theory, feminist theory, and a variety of other theories—to understand and analyze any topic of interest—in this case, the complicated subject of tourism.

Some topics I consider are:

- Is there a difference between travelers and tourists?

- What are the different kinds of tourism?

- Is there such a thing as the tourist "gaze"? If so, what is it and how does it function?

- How do theories about modernism and postmodernism relate to tourism?

- How does the exotic differ from the everyday?

- What motivates tourists? What gratifications are they seeking from their travels?

- What role does a tourist's willingness to tolerate risk play in his or her choice of places to visit?

- What role does myth play in tourism?

The remainder of the book uses semiotics and its allied disciplines to analyze some of the most important iconic destinations in the world and the role they play in the tourism industry. Most of these sites are UNESCO world heritage sites; the others are world-class tourism destinations. Except for the Gehry Guggenheim Museum in Bilbao, Spain, the Potala Palace in Lhasa, and the capital of Brazil, Brasilia, I've had the pleasure of visiting all of the sites discussed in this book, so I write with first-hand knowledge of most of the tourist icons I deal with.

At the beginning of each chapter, to enrich your understanding of the complexities of studying tourism, I provide quotations that either deal with theoretical matters or with the iconic building or place being analyzed. And in the chapters, I provide quotations from important writers and tourism scholars sharing what they have to say about tourism. Reading this book will have a number of outcomes: first, you will learn about some of the theories and issues that play an important role in tourism research and scholarship, and second, you will learn about the role the world's most significant iconic buildings and places play in the decision making of tourists, in the tourism industry, and in the societies in which the tourist icons are found. Finally, you will learn about some of the most important tourist destinations that you might want to visit when you travel. At the end of the book I have provided a list of applications and exercises that deal with the information in this book.

Theorizing Tourism: Analyzing Iconic Destinations by Arthur Asa Berger, 9–11.
© 2013 Left Coast Press, Inc. All rights reserved.

What gives value to travel is fear. It is the fact that, at a certain moment, when we are so far from our own country...we are seized by a vague fear, and this instinctive desire to go back to the protection of old habits. This is the most obvious benefit of travel. At that moment we are feverish but also porous, so that the slightest touch makes us quiver to the depths of our being....This is why we should not say that we travel for pleasure. There is no pleasure in travelling, and I look upon it as an occasion for spiritual testing. Pleasure takes us away from ourselves the same way that distraction, as in Pascal's use of the world, takes us away from God. Travel, which is like a greater and grave science, brings us back to ourselves.

Albert Camus, *Notebooks, 1935–1942.*

I should have liked to live in the age of real travel, when the spectacle on offer had not yet been blemished, contaminated, and confounded; then I could have seen Lahore not as I saw it, but as it appeared to "Bernier, Tavernier, Manucci"....There's no end, of course, to such conjectures. When was the right moment to see India? At what period would the study of the Brazilian savage have yielded the purest satisfaction and the savage himself have been at his peak?...The alternative is inescapable: either I am a traveller in ancient times, and faced with a prodigious spectacle which would be almost entirely unintelligible to me and might, indeed, provoke me to mockery or disgust; or I am a traveller of our own day, hastening in search of a vanished reality.

Claude Lévi-Strauss, *Tristes Tropiques: an anthropological study of primitive societies in Brazil.*

Chapter 1

Studying Tourism

Over the course of humanity's long history, we've built many remarkable buildings and places that travelers have sought out—for a variety of reasons. Some, like the French anthropologist Lévi-Strauss, travel in search of a "vanished" reality. Others, as Albert Camus suggests, travel to test themselves. In some cases, people are on religious pilgrimages and visit sites that have a sacred importance. Thus, for example, several million Muslims visit Mecca every year, and many Roman Catholics visit the Vatican. In other cases, travelers want to see the most famous and celebrated buildings because of their aesthetic and historic significance. That helps explain the importance of the Eiffel Tower, the Great Wall of

China, the Frank Gehry Guggenheim Museum in Bilbao, Spain, and the Taj Mahal to tourists.

Sometimes people travel for a number of different reasons. They may be on a religious pilgrimage, but they might also visit famous buildings, go to culturally important places, and conduct business—all at the same time. They are all tourists, even though some of them may describe themselves or think of themselves as "travelers" rather than tourists, since there are certain negative connotations to the term "tourist," especially the term "mass tourist." An American historian, Daniel Boorstin, differs with me on this matter. He argues, in his book *The Image,* that modern American tourists tend to be shallow individuals who are essentially in search of entertainment and are satisfied by the fake "pseudo-event" experiences sold to them by the tourist industry. He explains (1961:79–80):

> The modern American tourist now fills his experience with pseudo-events. He has come to expect both more strangeness and more familiarity than the world naturally offers. He has come to believe that he can have a lifetime of adventure in two weeks and all the thrills of risking his life without any real risk at all. He expects that the exotic and the familiar can be made to order: that a nearby vacation spot can give him Old World charm, and that if he chooses the right accommodations, he can have the comforts of home in the heart of Africa.

Boorstin develops his argument a few pages later when he contrasts the *traveler,* a person presumably rich, well-born, and able, with the middle-class *tourist.* He writes (1961:84–85):

> Formerly travel required long planning, large expense, and great investments of time. It involved risks to health or even to life. The traveler was active. Now he became passive. Instead of an athletic exercise, travel became a spectator sport. This change can be described in a word. It was the decline of the traveler and the rise of the tourist....Our American dictionary now defines a tourist as "a person who makes a pleasure trip" or "a person who makes a tour, especially for pleasure....The traveler... was working at something: the tourist is a pleasure-seeker. The traveller was active: he went strenuously in search of people, of adventure, of experience. The tourist is passive: he expects interesting things to happen to him. He goes sightseeing.

Boorstin offers a number of distinctions between travelers and tourists, as the chart below shows.

TRAVELERS	TOURISTS
working at something	pleasure seeker
active	passive
searches for adventure, people	expects things to happen to him
wants authenticity	likes pseudo-events, entertainment

There is some question about how valid Boorstin's argument is. I would suggest that Boorstin is an elitist who is contrasting nineteenth century travel, which was the realm of wealthy people, with contemporary twentieth and twenty-first century tourism, which is now largely a middle-class mass phenomenon. I will deal with some of the topics Boorstin mentions, such as pseudo-events or, in other language, simulations and the exotic, in various chapters in this book.

From my perspective, for all practical purposes, travelers are tourists and tourists are travelers. It is only at the extremes that they differ in important ways: the mass tourists who never leave their tourist "bubbles" are at one extreme and the lone travelers who do everything on their own and, in some cases, for some period of time, "go native" are at the other extreme.

Defining Tourism

The term "tourism" comes from the Greek term *tornos,* which means lathe or device for making a circle, so tourists are people who go somewhere and then return back home or to wherever they started. The World Tourist Organization (WTO) defines tourism as follows: "It comprises the activities of persons traveling to and staying in places outside their usual environment for not more than one consecutive year for leisure, business and other purposes not related to the exercise of an activity remunerated from within the place visited" (www.world-tourism.org/statistics/tsa_project/TSA%20depth/chapters/ch3-1.htm).

This definition is somewhat limited, in that people often combine business and pleasure when they travel, so I prefer to offer a broader understanding of tourism. Unless one travels purely for business purposes, does nothing else but conduct business, and then returns home, one is a tourist. As I argued earlier, generally speaking, tourists are travelers and travelers are tourists.

International tourism, which is the kind of tourism I deal with in this book, has, I suggest, the following characteristics:

- It is *temporary*, usually for a relatively short period of time.

- It is *voluntary*, done by choice.

- It is done in *foreign* lands or places outside one's usual environment.

- It is tied to *leisure* and *pleasure* and *consumer culture*.

- It is done for *pleasure*, *entertainment*, and related considerations.

- It is *not primarily involved with business* and earning money while abroad.

- It is based on a *round trip*, tied to a return to one's point of origin

- It is made possible by *technological developments* in travel and communication.

- It is a *mass phenomenon*, done by large numbers of people.

The fact that, according to the World Tourism Organization, there are around a billion international trips a year by tourists suggests how big the tourism industry is. Some international trips are only from one country to a neighboring country, such as from Thailand to Laos or from France to Belgium, which it is not much of a trip, though it still counts as international tourism. Many international trips, however, are "long haul" trips that involve long flights, sometimes two or three flights, to get to a site of interest. For example, a friend of mine who flew from San Francisco to South Africa told me it took him thirty-four hours from his house in San Francisco to get to his hotel in South Africa.

We have to be careful about tourism statistics; they are quite unreliable. As Bob McKercher explains (personal communication):

> Official statistics count the number of border crossings, rather than the number of individuals who travel. Thus, the same person could be counted numerous times during the same trip. When my friends came over from Canada, they were counted five times: entering Hong Kong; leaving Hong Kong and entering Macau; leaving Macau and reentering Hong Kong; leaving Hong Kong and entering China; leaving China

and reentering Hong Kong. Thus, in the course of one trip, the group of nine was counted 45 times. The issue is especially prevalent in western Europe where countries are small and therefore people are likely to cross borders repeatedly. Also, long haul tourists are far more likely to engage in multicountry trips than short-haul visitors. The long and short of it is that no one really knows how many actual tourists there are, even though we know that close to 1 billion border crossings were recorded.

So the billion international tourism arrivals that took place in 2011 may be a bit inflated.

The way I have chosen to deal with tourism is by analyzing or deconstructing the places international tourists visit, the famous buildings and places that act as magnets and draw people to them. When we watch television, we usually don't just turn on the set and watch whatever is on. We watch specific programs. The same applies to tourism. We travel to specific places—usually destinations that have attractions we want to see. These attractions are what I describe as global icons, and this book focuses upon destination tourism, and in many cases heritage tourism, though it deals with other matters as well.

Global Icons

[The United Nations Education, Scientific and Culture Organization's] World Heritage List includes 936 properties forming part of the cultural and natural heritage which the World Heritage Committee considers as having outstanding universal value. These include 725 cultural, 183 natural and 28 mixed properties in 153 States Parties. As of November 2011, 188 States Parties have ratified the World Heritage Convention. whc.unesco.org/en/about/.

The criteria for inclusion in the list of World Heritage Sites follow—taken from the UNESCO internet site (whc.unesco.org/en/list):

   i. to represent a masterpiece of human creative genius;
   ii. to exhibit an important interchange of human values, over a span of time or within a cultural area of the world, on developments in architecture or technology, monumental arts, town-planning or landscape design;
   iii. to bear a unique or at least exceptional testimony to a cultural tradition or to a civilization which is living or which has disappeared;

iv. to be an outstanding example of a type of building, architectural or technological ensemble or landscape which illustrates (a) significant stage(s) in human history;

v. to be an outstanding example of a traditional human settlement, land-use, or sea-use which is representative of a culture (or cultures), or human interaction with the environment especially when it has become vulnerable under the impact of irreversible change;

vi. to be directly or tangibly associated with events or living traditions, with ideas, or with beliefs, with artistic and literary works of outstanding universal significance. (The Committee considers that this criterion should preferably be used in conjunction with other criteria);

vii. to contain superlative natural phenomena or areas of exceptional natural beauty and aesthetic importance;

viii. to be outstanding examples representing major stages of earth's history, including the record of life, significant on-going geological processes in the development of landforms, or significant geomorphic or physiographic features;

ix. to be outstanding examples representing significant on-going ecological and biological processes in the evolution and development of terrestrial, fresh water, coastal and marine ecosystems and communities of plants and animals;

x. to contain the most important and significant natural habitats for in-situ conservation of biological diversity, including those containing threatened species of outstanding universal value from the point of view of science or conservation.

This list of criteria is quite large and deals with many topics, covering everything from city centers and architectural masterpieces to places of historical significance or extreme natural beauty. These criteria provide a justification for my inclusion of the various iconic buildings and places in this book: they are all of global cultural, historical, and even, in some cases, political significance, and most of them are on the list of 936 UNESCO World Heritage Sites.

Getting cited as a UNESCO World Heritage Site confers many economic advantages on a tourist site, and there is considerable competition to be named one. Once a site is included on the UNESCO World

Heritage list, it attracts many tourists who otherwise might not have visited it. There are questions about how some sites got on the list, and there might be an element of politics involved in the way UNESCO decides which sites to name. Whatever the case, being named a UNESCO World Heritage Site makes a site or building "world class" and thus the object of interest to many tourists. If you examine the list of criteria that UNESCO uses, you will notice terms such as "significant," "masterpiece," "outstanding," "most important," and "unique." Thus, these sites are all, UNESCO suggests, superlative ones and, as such, presumably worth the effort and expense involved in getting to see them.

We can track the location of many UNESCO sites by considering the countries that tourists visit the most. What follows is a list, for 2010, of the ten most popular countries for international tourists:

COUNTRY	TOURISTS (in Millions of Visitors)
France	76
United States	59
China	56
Spain	52
Italy	43
United Kingdom	28
Turkey	27
Germany	26
Malaysia	24
Mexico	22

International Tourism Visitors Statistics
(UNWTO World Tourism Barometer)

We can see from this list that international tourism is a big business in many countries, since tourists spend money on their trips. They spend money on travel, housing, dining, shopping, and visits to tourist sites which have iconic significance. These countries have a large proportion of the UNESCO World Heritage Sites, though they have other attractions as well. In 2011, the tourism industry employed 100 million people and tourists spent more than 1.2 trillion dollars, making it the largest industry in the world (www.wttc.org/site_media/uploads/downloads/traveltourism2011.pdf).

Though people have different reasons for being tourists, they are all in search of some kind of pleasure, some kind of payoff. The quotations that begin this chapter suggest that travel is a complicated matter and that it is related to unconscious drives and desires that motivate us to wander around the world. Claude Lévi-Strauss, a famous French anthropologist, lamented that he could not travel the way adventurers traveled before the age of mass travel.

An American professor, Dean MacCannell, sees the tourist as the archetype of modern man and woman. As he explains in his influential book *The Tourist: A New Theory of the Leisure Class* (1976:1):

> "TOURIST" is used to mean two things in this book. It designates actual tourists: sightseers, mainly middle-class, who are at the moment deployed throughout the entire world in search of experience. I want this book to serve as a sociological study of this group. But I should make it known that, from the beginning, I intended something more. The tourist is an actual person, or real people are actually tourists. At the same time, "the tourist" is one of the best models available for modern-man-in-general. I am equally interested in "the tourist" in this second, metasociological sense of the term. Our first apprehension of modern civilization, it seems to me, emerged in the mind of the tourist.

MacCannell's book is informed by semiotic theory, for tourists are, without realizing what they are doing, seeing or "processing" the places they see as applied semioticians. Modifying a dictum by Charles Peirce, one of the founding fathers of semiotics, we may say for a tourist, *a site* (Peirce wrote "a sign") *represents something to somebody*. I will discuss semiotics in more detail in the next chapter.

National Styles of Tourism: Japanese Tourists in Bali—A Case Study

As one might expect, tourists from different countries have different modes of travel—generally ones that are congruent with their national character. For example, Japanese tourists in Bali almost always take package tours that have very rigid schedules. In his book *Bali and Beyond*, Shinji Yamashita describes the "typical" Japanese tourist visit to Bali. It begins with a ten hour flight from Japan as part of a five-day group package tour. The schedule for these five days, adapted from material in his book, is:

Day 1: Arriving in late afternoon or evening and settling in.

Day 2: Sightseeing, purchasing souvenirs, and attending a *Barong dance.*

Day 3: Visiting craft villages such as Caulk or Mass or Bud. (In the evening they generally take advantage of two popular tour options: they watch the *kecak* dance and have a lobster dinner.)

Day 4: Flying to Yogyakarta to visit the temple at Borodudur and returning to Bali that evening.

Day 5: Devoting leisure time to wandering around, buying souvenirs before taking a night flight back to Japan.

According to Yamashita, Japanese tourists are highly programmed and are generally away from their hotels from early in the morning until late in the evening. This means that they don't get to enjoy the sea view hotel rooms they usually book. Yamashita adds that tourism is a kind of "work" for Japanese who feel upset if they miss something (that means, they are unable to photograph it). Westerners, he adds, generally come for stays of one or two weeks and thus can be much more relaxed about their sightseeing and shopping. They also come, he writes, to "listen" and question rather than see. Japanese tourists account for 20 percent of the tourists in Bali but account for 50 percent of the money spent on souvenirs. So we have to consider the national character of tourists (in Japan, gift-giving after foreign travel is very important)—doing so helps us comprehend why understanding tourist behavior is such a complicated matter. The way people from different countries spend time and money as tourists, we see, is connected to their national character.

Studying Tourism at Universities

Many universities now have large departments that deal with various aspects of tourism—everything from marketing to hotel management, and there are dozens of scholarly journals that deal with various aspects of tourism. There are, it is estimated, something like 3,000 universities that offer courses in tourism and hospitality studies. One of the largest and most important schools of tourism is the School of Hotel and Tourism Management at Hong Kong Polytechnic University. According to the dean of the school, Kaye Chon, it has 50 faculty members from 18 countries, 1,300 undergraduate students, 300 students working for MA degrees and 30 doctoral students. Chon, says he expects to have 75 faculty members in the near future. According to Bob McKercher, who was kind enough to supply me with these statistics about tourism and hospitality education: Hong Kong has 18 universities and China has 1,200 institutions of higher education that offer courses in tourism. Between January 2000 and December 2004, McKercher adds, more than 3,200 scholars wrote or co-authored articles on tourism that were published in refereed journals (personal communication).

In the United States, Cornell's tourism school, founded in 1922, is one of the oldest and most prestigious universities offering courses in tourism; it is estimated that there are around 400 universities in America teaching the subject and 50,000 students majoring in tourism and hospitality studies. In addition to scholars who are members of schools of tourism, psychologists and semioticians and sociologists and many other scholars not directly involved with tourism departments and schools often deal with aspects of tourism in their research and writings (www.hotcoursesabroad.com).

A Typology of Kinds of Tourism

There are, I would suggest, very few "plain vanilla" tourists. Every tourist, at least from the perspective of tourist scholars, engages in one or more kinds of tourism. What follows is a list of the most important categories of tourism. The term "typology" means the study of types and involves classification systems by which we seek to organize knowledge. We must recognize that although tourists may travel for one reason, they can partake of other kinds of tourism as well. Here are some of the more important kinds of tourism. In many cases, these kinds of tourism involve long-haul international travel.

CULTURAL TOURISM

This involves travel to sites of cultural significance, often for the historical importance of the site. Examples would be visiting the Taj Mahal or Angkor Wat. Cultural tourists also visit museums, go to symphony concerts, operas, ballets, theaters, native "folk" dances, and other "elite" forms of the arts. Visits to the homes of great writers is also an important form of cultural tourism. This kind of tourism is generally a major component of mass tourism and "free-individual tourism" (people who made their own arrangements were labeled FITS—Free Individual Tourists—on a river cruise I took in Ukraine).

HERITAGE TOURISM

Sometimes called "Diaspora tourism," this kind of tourism, narrowly speaking, involves people who visit sites that are bound up with their own heritage. Thus, Italian-Americans visit Italy and Jewish people visit Israel because these places are tied to their heritage. But it can also involve visiting sites of "universal" cultural significance. UNESCO defines cultural heritage as:

> The practices, representations, expressions, knowledge, skills—as well as the instruments, objects, artefacts and cultural spaces, associated therewith—that communities, groups, and, in some cases, individuals recognize as part of their cultural heritage. This intangible cultural heritage, transmitted from generation to generation, is constantly recreated by communities and groups in response to their environment, their interaction with nature and their history, and provides them with a sense of identity and continuity, thus promoting respect for cultural diversity and human creativity. (UNESCO Convention for the Safeguarding of the Intangible Cultural Heritage)

From my perspective, heritage tourism is connected to cultural tourism, except that, in the narrowest sense, it involves a personal relationship, however distant, to the sites being visited.

ADVENTURE TOURISM

Adventure tourists go to countries where they can hike in beautiful forests, run white water rapids in rubber boats, climb mountains (sometimes at their peril), and have other kinds of adventures. There is a difference between "hard adventure travel," which involves trekking, mountain climbing, and so on and "soft adventure travel," which might involve a jeep safari and then a return to a luxury lodge at night.

SUSTAINABLE TOURISM

Many adventure tourists are eco-tourists who are vitally concerned with maintaining the ecology of places they visit and preventing the degradation of sites caused by too many tourist visits. The term "ecotourism" has been abused, so many tourism scholars now prefer to use "sustainable" or "responsible" tourism.

GASTRONOMIC TOURISM

These tourists are "foodies" who are interested in the cuisines of different countries and focus their attention on famous restaurants or food specialties of different cities or regions in a country. There are many gastronomy tours designed for this kind of tourist, and many cities offer tourists half-day and day-long courses that teach people who attend them how to cook various specialties.

DRUG TOURISM

Some tourists travel to cities, such as Amsterdam, where certain drugs can be used legally, and tourists, then, have easy access to drugs. Amsterdam is now doing things to eliminate drug tourism, but there are many other cities and countries where drugs can be obtained with relative ease.

SPORTS TOURISM

The main reason sports tourists travel is to see sporting events of importance to them—often internationally significant events such as Wimbledon, the World Series, important football/soccer games like the World Cup, and the Super Bowl. The behavior of some international tourists/fans, commonly called football hooligans, at soccer games in foreign countries has become a major problem for the management of the teams, the stadiums where the games are held, and the police. Because fans of these games become excited and sometimes because they have too much to drink, occasionally there are fights, riots, and even killings at these events.

GAMBLING TOURISM

Tourists go to cities like Las Vegas and Macau to gamble. The term for this activity now is "gaming," since "gambling" has negative connotations. Las Vegas pretends it is a city for families, but the heart of the tourist industry there involves gambling. Las Vegas facilitates gambling and other behaviors that may not be typical of people who visit the city by arguing "What happens in Las Vegas stays in Las Vegas."

SHOPPING TOURISM

Tourists generally shop when they travel—to bring back souvenirs, to take advantage of bargains, and to find out things about the places they are visiting. But some tourists only travel to shop—visiting shopping meccas like Dubai or the Mall of America, and when they are done shopping, they return home.

SEXUAL TOURISM

Many tourists visit countries in search of sexual partners, and many cities have districts to accommodate this kind of tourist. In some cultures, people of both sexes have different attitudes toward sexual relations than are found in some Western European countries, though sexual tourism is all-pervasive. Some cities, such as Amsterdam, have "red light' districts, and other cities, such as Bangkok, have a highly developed sexual tourism industry. Unfortunately, a small number of sexual tourists are predators who travel in search of young children. A recent article in the *New York Times* used the term "brothel tourism," which may be considered a form of sexual tourism.

MEDICAL TOURISM

In recent decades, this kind of tourism has grown considerably, since it is possible now to have medical procedures and dental work done in Brazil, Thailand, India, and many other countries for much less than in the United States or Western European countries. In some cases, people take a trip to Thailand, for example, for cultural tourism or sexual tourism (or both), but also have some medical work done, as long as they are there. There are now companies in the United States that facilitate medical tourism and arrange everything for the medical tourist. I would include going to spas or having massages as a light form of medical tourism. Sometimes medical tourism can be problematic. In Hong Kong, now, there is a problem caused by pregnant women from Mainland China who come to Hong Kong to have their babies, so they will have Hong Kong citizenship, which has many benefits. The medical clinics are over-run by these Mainland Chinese women, and pregnant Hong Kong women often have trouble finding room in a hospital to deliver their babies.

DISASTER TOURISM

Strange as it might seem, there are some tourists who travel to countries in search of disasters that have happened there. Some of these disaster tourists may travel to be of help, to the extent they can, and others are voyeurs, who take pleasure in seeing the destruction that has taken place in a city or other area. Doctors and nurses who travel to be of assistance in disaster areas are not disaster tourists. A subcategory of Disaster Tourism is Atrocity Tourism, which involves visits to places where atrocities have taken place, including the former World Trade Center and Nazi death camps in Germany and Poland.

Family Tourism

This kind of tourism involves travel to visit members of one's family, often for major life events like bar mitzvahs, communions, weddings, births, or deaths. During a recent trip to India, the hotel in which my wife and I were staying was closing to tourists the day we left because it was reserved for guests from all over India attending the wedding of the daughter of the hotel owner.

Religious Tourism

Many tourists travel for religious reasons. They go on pilgrimages, they travel to visit holy places, and they go to participate in religious celebrations. Every year, several million Muslims go to Mecca on the Haj—a trip that the Koran suggests all Muslims should take if they can afford to do so. Jewish and Christian tourists who visit Israel will almost always include the Western Wall in Jerusalem or the Church of the Nativity in Bethlehem on their itineraries. There are numerous Hindu, Buddhist, Jewish, Catholic and Muslim mosques, churches, temples, synagogues, wats, and other sites of interest to religious tourists.

As an example of what motivates religious tourists, let me quote from Samuel Jemsel (in Adler, 1930:329) who explains why he felt compelled to undertake his holy travels:

> I was possessed by a violent and insatiable desire to visit the places of God...as I had learnt that eminent men such as Rabbi Isaac and Rabbi Solomon Levi had also been inflamed with the desire of accomplishing the holy journey. I, being urged on like them by a sort of divine instinct, did not lose sight of the execution of my project: I would not have suffered myself to be turned aside from it by any reason whatsoever. The desire to set out which had formed itself in my mind was so violent that it was impossible for me to remain in my own home, or to go about my accustomed business.

Jemsel is an extreme case, but there is a passion found in many religious tourists that helps explain why they are willing to undertake long and sometimes arduous and expensive trips to go on a pilgrimage or attend a religious event.

Conference Tourism

Every profession has conferences in which important figures in some profession or industry give lectures on topics of interest to people attending the conference. In addition, people in a profession meet with others in their field to discuss matters of mutual concern. At many conferences it is possible for attendees to look for a job. There are annual national conferences for scholars in most fields, as well as regional conferences. In the technology area, conferences are important because new products are often introduced. Attending conferences may be seen as business travel, but many people who attend such conferences also take advantage of the cultural and other benefits of the locations where the conferences are held. A relatively recent development in this kind of tourism is called MICE or Meetings and Incentives Tourism, which involves corporate incentive trips.

Voluntarism Tourism aka Philanthropic Tourism

Doctors, dentists, and nurses who voluntarily go to poor countries to treat people and tourists who go to work on archaeological digs are what I would describe as voluntarist tourists. The basic motivation of these tourists is to help others.

Educational Tourism

Students who take a junior year abroad or a semester abroad to study in foreign countries as well as those who take short courses and summer courses in foreign institutions are involved in educational tourism. Older adults who participate in Elderhostel programs in different cities or in foreign countries or who take special courses in foreign countries are also educational tourists.

Events Tourism

This kind of tourism involves travel to events of interest and significance, such as the Mardi Gras in Rio or New Orleans or the wedding of royals in Great Britain. It might also cover spring breaks at beaches in Mexico and other countries where college and university students congregate in large numbers.

Beach Tourism

Many tourists go to places with beautiful beaches, where they can enjoy swimming (sea, sun, sand, sex, and shopping tourism) and just relax without having to expend the amount of energy and effort that some other kinds of tourism involve.

We can see from this list that there are many kinds of tourism for people with a variety of interests and, as I explained earlier, it is not unusual for people to engage in different kinds of tourism at different stages in their life cycles. And, of course, frequently tourists engage in several kinds of tourism in one trip.

Categories of Tourists

Having just dealt with kinds of tourism, let me now deal with a related topic—some classifications of types or kinds of tourists. First, I will deal with two of the most well known and influential theories about categories of tourists, and then I will offer a theory I have developed based on grid-group theory. The first, and one of the most important, classification systems was developed by an Israeli sociologist, Erik Cohen, who has written many articles and books on tourism. In his article, "Toward a Sociology of International Tourism" (in Kotler et al., 1999:662) Cohen discusses what he describes as organized mass tourists:

> The organized mass tourist is the least adventurous and remains largely confined to his "environmental bubble" throughout his trip. The guided tour, conducted in an air conditioned bus, traveling at high speed through a streaming countryside, represents the prototype of the organized mass tourist. This tourist type buys a package tour as if it were just another commodity in the modern mass market. The itinerary for his trip is fixed in advance, and all his stops are well-prepared and guided: he makes almost no decisions for himself and stays almost exclusively in the microenvironment of his home country. Familiarity is at a maximum, novelty at a minimum.

Cohen lists four kinds of tourists in his article: the Organized Mass Tourist, the Individual Mass Tourist, the Explorer, and the Drifter. Organized Mass Tourists book tours with travel agencies that take care of most of their needs—hotels, transportation, guides, and so on. They are firmly in the "tourist bubble." Individual Mass Tourists makes their travel arrangements using a travel agency but retain a certain amount of control over their time and itinerary, and venture out of the "tourist bubble" to interact with people more than Organized Mass Tourists do. Explorers make all of their own arrangements and want to experience the richness of the cultures they visit, but they don't want to completely remove themselves from the bubble. They may, for example, stay at very fine hotels.

Drifters abandon the bubble and go native, attempting—to the extent they can—to live the way natives in the countries they visit do. Mass tourism, Cohen suggests, is made up mostly of Organized Mass Tourists and Individual Mass Tourists, with Explorers and Drifters comprising a relatively small percentage of tourists. Some cruise lines now emphasize the "bubble" quality of their ships—a respite with familiar food and the desired comforts after a day visiting exotic sites.

I would describe myself as a "soft Explorer" tourist since my wife and I generally make all our own travel arrangements, though we generally stay at nice hotels or in apartments that we book through the internet. We have visited more than fifty countries and have only been what Cohen describes as "Organized Mass Tourists" in countries where it is extremely difficult and not cost-effective to travel on one's own. There is, in the tourism industry now, a move away from Group Inclusive Tours (GIT) to Free Independent Travel (FIT).

Another typology of tourists, one of the earliest and most influential, was developed by Stanley Plog. He argues, in an essay "Why Destinations Rise and Fall in Popularity," that there are five kinds of tourists based on their fearfulness and adventurousness: Psychocentric, Near Psychocentric, Mid-Centric, Near Allocentric, and Allocentric. We can see these kinds of tourists on the chart below:

TOLERATE RISK   FEARFUL OF RISK

•   •   •   •   •
_____

Allocentric   Near Allocentric   Mid-Centric   Near Psychocentric   Psychocentric

Allocentric tourists tolerate risk and are adventurous. According to Plog, allocentric tourists—backpackers and explorers—discover new tourism sites of interest, and as these sites become developed, they start attracting tourists from the middle of continuum. When the sites are well developed and have all the creature comforts many tourists demand, they attract Psychocentric tourists.

My own contribution to classifying tourists is based on grid-group theory. The analysis that follows is based on one I made in my book *Deconstructing Travel,* but is considerably modified. My discussion of tourism here draws upon the work of political scientist Aaron Wildavsky and social anthropologist Mary Douglas, with whom he often collaborated. Wildavsky said that grid-group or cultural theory tries to help people answer two basic questions—one involves identity: *Who am I?* and the other involves action: *What should I do?* Wildavsky writes (in his article "A Cultural Theory of Preference Formation" in Berger, 1989:25):

> The question of identity may be answered by saying that individuals belong to a strong group, a collective that makes decisions binding on all members or that their ties to others are weak in that their choices bind only themselves. The question of action is answered by responding that the individual is subject to many or few prescriptions, a free spirit or tightly constrained. The strength or weakness of group boundaries and the numerous or few, varied or similar prescriptions binding or freeing individuals are the components of their culture.

There are, then, Wildavsky suggests, four political cultures—and, in the economic realm, as Douglas argues, four consumer cultures—that arise from the answers to these two questions—am I in a group with weak or strong boundaries and few or many rules and prescriptions. You get what Wildavsky calls hierarchical, individualist, egalitarian and fatalist/apathetic cultures. We can see how these cultures are formed out of the strength and weakness of group boundaries and the numbers and kinds of rules and prescription. Below I list the four political and consumer cultures that lead to four kinds of tourists: hierarchists, egalitarians, individualists, and fatalists.

CULTURE GROUP	BOUNDARIES	NUMBER OF PRESCRIPTIONS
Hierarchists	strong	numerous and varied
Egalitarians (Enclavists)	strong	few and weak
Individualists	weak	few and weak
Fatalists (Isolates)	weak	numerous and varied

Elitist tourists, grid-group theory suggests, search for hierarchy and obtain it when they travel by choosing luxury cruises or other luxury forms of travel, where they will find, they can assume—due to the cost of their travel—people like them. Luxury tours and everything associated with this kind of travel help them maintain social distance from members of the other consumer cultures. Individualist tourists, not wanting anyone to tell them what to do, will travel independently, booking their hotels and other aspects of their trips through their travel agents or on their own, using the internet. They tend to avoid packaged tours.

Egalitarians will focus their travel on cultural matters, nature preservation, and sustainable tourism, wanting to do all they can to preserve nature and to show their links with people everywhere; they will avoid, to the extent they can, the kinds of tourism liked by Elitists and Individualists. Fatalist tourists, who are generally at the bottom of the financial totem-pole and have few resources, will take trips by automobile or bus or short excursions by rail or air. One reason why certain travel experiences may not be pleasurable for some tourists is that, by chance, they made the wrong kind of travel arrangements and ended up with people from a different and antagonistic consumer culture or "lifestyle" (the term Douglas uses).

Wildavsky and Douglas force us to consider that the various analyses of travel and tourism as a kind of consumption made by scholars who are unaware of the importance of the different consumer cultures may be overly simplistic and inadequate. If we want to know why people choose to travel the way they do, according to Wildavsky and Douglas, we shouldn't probe their minds and psyches, but should find out to which consumer culture they belong, since it is cultural alignment that explains preferences in politics and tourism and all other forms of consumption, including shopping—which, research indicates, is one of the main things people do when they are tourists.

We can see from my discussion of these models that there are different ways of classifying tourists, just as there are many different kind of tourism. One problem with most typologies is that while they are interesting and lead to insights of some importance, there are an infinite number of possibilities that one can use in creating a typology. The advantage of the Wildavsky and Douglas analysis is that it is based on their grid and group dimensions. As Michael Thompson, Richard Ellis, and Aaron Wildavsky explain in their book *Cultural Theory* (1990:261):

> We are in agreement with Robert Brown that "when someone produces a 'bulky system,' he must also answer the implied question 'A system for what?' He cannot merely rely on 'It organizes the data.' *Any* criterion will organize data—will order items in classes—but only some classifications are scientifically useful." That is why we insist that typologies must be based on dimensions that form categories, not on categories by themselves.

I would suggest that we consider the various tourism typologies (and there are many others that I didn't deal with) as all offering different perspectives and insights into the kinds of tourists, their psyches, their motivations, and the role that their cultural group plays in shaping their behavior; thus, they are all of considerable value, even if they don't meet the standards of grid-group theorists.

Controversies Involved with Tourism and Tourism Research

As might be expected, there are many controversies involved with tourism and tourism research. In the material that follows I will deal with a few of the most important controversies in the field. Scholarly tourism journals are full of articles that discuss topics related to tourism and issues that shape tourist behavior all over the world. One of the most controversial involves the matter of authenticity and its role in the psyches of tourists and the tourism industry.

Authenticity

The word "modern" comes from the Latin word *modernus,* which was used to differentiate the pagan era from the Christian era. Modernism dominated our architecture, the arts, and Western culture from approximately 1900 until 1960, when it was replaced by postmodernism. Postmodernism develops at the same time that consumer capitalism becomes dominant, and thus postmodernism is associated with consumer culture and mass consumption that dominate fashion and shape people's lifestyles. We live now, culture theorists argue, in a world dominated by media, images, and simulations of reality. Like so many belief systems, postmodernism is intimately connected to the system it rejected and replaced—modernism.

One topic of interest to tourism scholars, which I alluded to earlier, involves the matter of authenticity. Some tourism scholars believe that tourists, in general, are modernists in search of authenticity; they want to experience the "real" thing when they are abroad and want a "deep" immersion in foreign cultures. Other scholars suggest that in postmodern times, tourists are not in search of authenticity, but of pseudo-events, entertainment, and amusement. We can see the difference between modernist and postmodernist tourists in this chart:

MODERNIST TOURISTS	POSTMODERNIST TOURISTS
authenticity	amusement and entertainment
the "real" thing	hyperreality
natural	artificial

Thus, Erik Cohen, who I quoted earlier, explains:

Recent developments in tourism make the issue of "authenticity," for various reasons, increasingly less relevant. Perhaps the most obvious reason is that the Western domination of the tourist system is in the contemporary world increasingly challenged under the impact of a rapidly growing number of travelers from non-Western counties. These come principally from the wealthy Middle East, and from Asia, where the new middle classes of Japan, China, India, South Korea and Thailand developed a taste for international travel.

    Students of tourism have for long been oblivious to the significance of this rising trend for the sociological analysis of tourism. We know little about the motivations and desires of the growing numbers of non-Western tourists; but it is reasonable to assume, that they did not share the Westerners' "art of travel" in the past; nor are they necessarily impelled by a quest for "authenticity" at present. The question, what are the culturally justified motives for travel of non-Western travelers, and how these help to fashion their style of travel, and their choices of destinations and activities, is one of the major issues, presently facing the sociological study of tourism. (Cohen, 2008:331)

This topic remains a controversial one in tourism studies, and is connected to the importance of postmodernism, since postmodernist thought focuses on simulations and simulacra and is not terribly concerned with what is real and what is fake. Tourists, in general, may not be concerned with authenticity, but for a large number of tourists, seeing the Taj Mahal means something to them because it is the real thing and not an imitation.

Sociologist Ning Wang discusses the question of authenticity in his book *Tourism and Modernity*. He writes (2000:55):

Implied in the approaches of postmodernism is justification of the contrived, the copy, and the imitation. One of the most interesting responses to this postmodern cultural condition is Cohen's recent justification of contrived attractions in tourism. According to him, postmodern tourists have become less concerned with the authenticity of the original... Two reasons can be identified. First, if the cultural sanction of the modern tourist has been the "quest for authenticity," then that of the postmodernist tourist is a "playful search for enjoyment" or an "aesthetic enjoyment of surfaces." Secondly, the postmodern tourist becomes more sensitive to the impact of tourism upon fragile host communities or tourist sites. Staged authenticity thus helps project a fragile toured culture and community from disturbance by acting as a substitute for the original and keeping tourists away from it.

Wang suggests that postmodern tourists—which, nowadays, generally means most tourists—are not worried about authenticity and are more interested in being entertained and amused than seeing "authentic" tourist sites. This means that "staged" authenticity (or simulations for tourists) are perfectly acceptable to them. In addition, as Wang points out, these simulated attractions have a benefit for people living in places visited by tourists—they help fragile authentic tourist sites maintain themselves. As you can well imagine, this topic is the subject of considerable controversy among tourism scholars.

The Tourist Gaze

When tourists travel, they usually go sight-seeing (or from a semiotic perspective, sign-seeing). That is, they search out the places of most interest as far as having historically important and visually arresting sites or "photo opportunities"—along with other attributes such as a distinctive cuisine and opportunities for shopping. They also, so some theorists suggest, "gaze" at native people from a position of superiority.

John Urry, a British sociologist, offers this description of the tourist gaze in an article on "Globalizing the Tourist Gaze":

> One effect of mobile technologies is to change the nature of vision. The 'static' forms of the tourist gaze, such as that from 'the balcony vantage point', focuses on the two-dimensional shape, colours and details of the view that is laid out before one and can be moved around with one's eyes (Pratt, 1992: 222). Such a static gaze is paradigmatically captured through the still camera. By contrast, with what Schivelbusch terms a 'mobility of vision', there are swiftly passing panorama, a sense of multi-dimensional rush and the fluid interconnections of places, peoples and possibilities (1986: 66); similar to the onrushing images encountered on TV and film). There are a variety of tourist glances, the capturing of

sights in passing from a railway carriage, through the car windscreen, the steamship porthole or the camcorder viewfinder (see Larsen, 2001). As Schivelbusch argues: 'the traveller sees ... through the apparatus which moves him through the world. The machine and the motion it creates become integrated into his visual perception; thus he can only see things in motion.' (Osborne, 2000:168)

Tourists, according to "gaze" theorists, are concerned primarily with visually arresting places and with photographing them, rather than with interacting with people in places they visit.

This description of tourism is the subject of debate by other scholars who argue it is reductionistic. In her article "The Ideal Village: Interactions through Tourism in Central Anatolia" (in Abram et al., 1997) Hazel Tucker discusses commonly held views about the tourist gaze. She writes about typical tourist experiences in Goreme, a village in Central Turkey:

Analyses of tourism and tourist culture have tended to work through a purely visual framework, responding to the perpetual visualization in tourism-related discourses. Indeed, Urry (1990) argues that tourism is all about gazing upon particular scenes that are different from those encountered in everyday life. Furthermore, this view of tourism has led Urry to the conclusion that since postmodernity is marked by "the proliferation of images and symbols".... Tourism is coming home, since it is now possible "to *see* many of the typical objects of the tourist gaze.... in one's own living room, at the flick of a switch." (1997:107)

Tucker argues that Urry's notion, while popular, is simplistic and ignores the fact that many tourists actively seek interactions with people in the countries they visit and are not just interested in seeing sights and photographing them, even though the "moon-like" landscape in Goreme, Turkey, and other nearby towns is quite fantastic.

Tucker continues on with her discussion of the touristic gaze and suggests that tourists aren't the only ones who gaze (1997:25):

The power of the photographic gaze is evident both through the symbolic representations "captured" within the pictures and in the actual process of taking photographs. Here we return to the idea of Goreme's being a "living museum," through which the people of the village are gazed upon, appropriated and collected. When photographed, the villages of Goreme are rendered "objects".... in an existential sense, in which there is a constant battle to be subject or object in relation to the other.... However, whilst much has been written about the power gaze of tourists upon "others," the return gaze is not so often considered.

Tucker points out that during her stay in Goreme, the power of the gaze was not all one-sided in favor of the tourists and points out that the people of Goreme gazed back at tourists, and, because they were on their home territory and were in larger numbers than the tourists, often their gaze was more powerful, that is, more based on a sense of superiority, than that of the tourists.

It is, I would suggest, simplistic to assume that tourism is essentially visual and that the gaze of the tourist is not returned by the gaze of the native. There is a tourist gaze, because tourists seek places that are different—in some cases exotic—and the visual aspects of tourism are important, but so are other components of tourism. Tourists may become excited by people dressed in native costumes and gaze at them, but the natives, as often as not, gaze back. Each may find the other visually arresting and interesting.

Capturing the Experience: Tourists as Photographers

A social-psychologist, Stanley Milgram, wrote an article, "The Image Freezing Machine" (1976), that analyzed the importance of photography for tourists. We can think of photography as a method of taking the tourist gaze and making it a permanent part of the tourist's experience. Milgram suggests that the act of taking a picture is very much like the act of seeing itself. There is, he suggests, a trade-off between the passive enjoyment of a particular moment and the process of photographing it. The tourist who sees a beautiful scene generally stops to take a picture of it (or make a video of it), but this act may prevent the experience from being fully savored.

Milgram believes that the very meaning of travel becomes transformed by its photographic possibilities. Tourists seek out places not only for their beauty, but often because they provide suitable backgrounds for their pictures. A group of tourists, cameras hanging about their necks, he adds, sees its arrival at the Eiffel Tower as the consummation of a photographic quest. The place visited actually becomes secondary to its photographic potential. The value of our vacations depends, then, not only on what we might have experienced at a particular place but also on how it all comes out in the pictures.

The point that Milgram makes, that many people seem to go touring as if the only thing they wanted to do was find suitable photo opportunities, is well made, and probably does apply to some tourists. But on the tours that I've taken, the tourists were intent on having the best of both worlds—seeing beautiful places and taking photographs of these places, even if it meant taking a short break from gazing to take photographs. The development of video cameras, digital cameras, and point and shoot cameras has made the interruptions caused by capturing images much less significant now than it was in earlier years.

Some scholars see tourism photography, especially in third world countries, as an example of what might be described as "photographic colonialism." In *Culture and the Ad: Exploring Otherness in the World of Advertising,* William M. O'Barr discusses a book by Lisl Dennis, *How to Take Better Travel Photos.* He writes (1994:41):

> No matter how innocent Dennis may think her motives are, what she describes here is *photographic colonialism.* The similarities to economic and political colonialism are remarkable. We are instructed in this manual that people who live in other parts of the world are the raw materials for our photographs. Since they are neither using their own images nor seem to care or object, we may appropriate them.

O'Barr adds that Dennis's book suggests that for tourists, "all the world's a movie set" and that "the quaintness of people's lives exists, at least in part, as subject matter for the tourist's photographs" (1994:42).

Tourism and Consumer Cultures

Travel costs money. In earlier times, foreign travel was a luxury only enjoyed by elite classes, but now tourism is a "mass" phenomenon. Critics of American consumer culture quite naturally focus their attention on tourism since it is such an important force in our economy. After our purchases of houses, automobiles, and education (at the college and university level), our purchases of tours, ocean and river cruises, and other forms of tourism represent one of our largest areas of voluntary expenditure.

The French sociologist Jean Baudrillard suggests that there is an element of compulsion in tourism and all forms of consumption. Baudrillard explains that consumption must not be seen as a pleasure or a means of enjoyment, but as a *duty.* In a fascinating reversal of the Puritan ethic of hard work, now enjoyment and consumption are the required "business" of the typical person who is, so to speak, forced to have fun.

As Baudrillard writes in *The Consumer Society: Myths & Structures* (Sage, 1998:80):

> There is no question for the consumer, for the modern citizen, of evading this enforced happiness and enjoyment, which is the equivalent in the new ethics of the traditional imperative to labour and produce. Modern man spends less and less of his life in production within work and more and more of it in the *production* and continual innovation of his own needs and well-being. He must constantly see to it that all his potentialities, all his consumer capacities are mobilized. If he forgets to do so, he will be gently and insistently reminded that he has no right not to be happy. It is not, then, true that he is passive. He is engaged in—has to engage in—continual activity....Hence the revival of a *universal curiosity*....You have to try *everything,* for consumerist man is haunted by the fear of "missing" something, some form of enjoyment. You never know whether a particular encounter, a particular experience (Christmas in the Canaries, eel in whiskey, the Prado, LSD, Japanese-style love-making) will not elicit some "sensation." It is no longer desire, or even "taste," or a specific inclination that are [*sic*] at stake, but a generalized curiosity, driven by a vague sense of unease—it is the "fun morality" or the imperative to enjoy oneself, to exploit to the full one's potential for thrills, pleasure or gratification.

We see that travel and experiences of the differences that are found in various cultures play an important part in Baudrillard's analysis. Christmas in the Canaries is a somewhat exotic location that might help the consumer obtain the pleasures that are required of him, or, conversely, she can go to Madrid and visit the Prado, satisfying her need for culture and refinement in one of the great museums of the world. There is an element of compulsion to all this, as if tourists, as consumers, feel they *must* suck the marrow out of life, and see everything that is worth seeing and go every place that is worth visiting and eat everything that is worth eating.

Critics of consumer cultures argue that these cultures are privatistic. In them, people focus on indulging in their own personal desires and seeking their own gratifications with little regard for the needs of others in the societies in which they live. Travel becomes a kind of momentary escape from the monotony of everyday life and the problems we face at work and at home. With these issues and philosophical questions or problems in mind, let us turn to our last topic: the motivations found in tourism, and, more specifically, the psychological gratifications tourists obtain from international travel.

What Motivates Tourists? A Uses and Gratifications Approach

This analysis draws on a field of communications social science research known as "Uses and Gratifications Theory." A number of years ago, social scientists started asking people why they listened to certain radio programs, watched certain television programs, went to certain films, or read certain kinds of novels. From people's answers the scientists compiled a list of gratifications that the media provided the general public, a list that led to a focus for many years in media and communication studies on "Uses and Gratifications Research." I will adapt some of their findings and apply them to the gratifications that visits to certain iconic "world-class" tourist sites provide.

One reason many people travel is that they have generally purchased so many things that they don't need very much else in the way of material goods, and so they choose to travel to have interesting experiences and because they believe that travel, especially foreign travel, will broaden their perspectives and enrich their lives. That is a common theme in many books and articles on tourism, in general, and places of interest for tourists, in particular.

To See Beautiful Places

One of the pleasures of travel involves visiting beautiful cities, such as Paris or Venice, and natural locations such as the desert in Morocco, spectacular islands, and pristine beaches that we find spiritually uplifting and life enhancing.

To Satisfy Our Curiosity

Humans are naturally curious, and tourists are people who are able to travel to foreign lands to satisfy their curiosity about what life in other countries is like. Even tourists who visit foreign countries for short periods of time can get insights into what is distinctive about the cultures they are visiting if they are perceptive, and they can gain a sense of perspective on life's possibilities.

To Be Amused and Entertained

Tourists wish to have experiences that they will find entertaining and pleasurable. This might involve going to a restaurant in a foreign country, to a spectacle such as a bullfight in Spain, or watching a performance of folk dancing. One of the most important ways that tourists "entertain" themselves is by shopping for souvenirs—objects that will remind them of their experiences in foreign countries and which, as is sometimes the case, will be a bargain. These souvenirs are given to others as an expression of care or kept by tourists to help them remember their experiences.

To Gain a Sense of the Fellowship of Men and Women

Tourists usually derive a great deal of pleasure from interacting with people in other countries and gaining a sense of fellowship and community with them. Some tourism theorists suggest that these interactions, chance meetings that lead to "peak" experiences, are what tourists remember most about their visits.

To Participate in History

One thing that tourists gain when they travel is participation in history, which explains why they desire to be at important sporting events or visit places where great historical events took place or great historical figures lived and worked. The French philosopher Descartes said "traveling is like conversing with men of other centuries." People want to connect themselves to places and events of importance, and through tourism—visiting Freud's home or the Great Mosque in Istanbul or the Bastille—they can do so. This kind of tourism may represent an attempt to deal with the diffuse and subliminal anxiety most people have about the fact that, as J. William Fulbright once explained, our lives are minor events in the ongoing universe—except for us and our families and friends, that is.

To Obtain Outlets for Sexual Drives in a Guilt-Free Manner

Sexual tourism and sometimes sexual exploitation is an important element in the travel industry, even though governments in countries where it exists try (or claim they try) to curtail it. Many travelers feel that having sex outside monogamous relationships with the same sex, the opposite sex, or (unfortunately) children in foreign countries is not morally problematic. Even if sex is not directly involved, much tourism is related to sex: couples going on vacation to have sex with their partners, to have sex with people who aren't their partners, to find partners, or to gaze at people of other cultures whose behaviors and dress arouse them. We might suggest that there are various kinds of sexual gratifications found in tourism: sexual intercourse, gazing at beautiful women and handsome men, and, taking an expansive perspective on human sexuality, the oral gratifications people obtain eating strange foods in unusual settings.

This chapter has offered a survey of some of the more important topics involved with studying tourism and some of the more controversial ideas and theories in the field. My focus has been on tourism in general, and not with practical matters such as managing hotels or marketing tourist sites. Standard tourism textbooks consider these matters in considerable detail, as do many of the scholarly tourism journals. I deal with other matters of theoretical interest in the chapters on global icons. Like all fields, there are many debates by tourism scholars about every conceivable aspect of tourism—from tipping to forecasting the number of tourists who will visit a city like Hong Kong and where they will probably come from and how they will spend their money.

Most people are not aware of the size and importance of the tourism industry (now a one trillion dollar industry) and of the amount of research being conducted by scholars in tourism schools in colleges and universities all over the world. There are dozens of scholarly journals devoted to various aspects of tourism—marketing, hotel management, eco-tourism, theories of tourism, and so on. As tourism asserts itself as a major economic force in the world, universities are now recognizing tourism's importance and devoting more resources to its study.

Theorizing Tourism: Analyzing Iconic Destinations by Arthur Asa Berger, 12–41.

It seems a strange thing, when one comes to ponder over it, that a sign should leave its interpreter to supply part of its meaning; but the explanation of the phenomenon lies in the fact that the entire universe—not merely the universe of existents, but all that wider universe, embracing the universe of existents, as a part, the universe which we are all accustomed to refer to as "the truth"—that all this universe is perfused with signs, if it not composed exclusively of signs.

C.S. Peirce; Epigraph in T. Sebeok, *A Perfusion of Signs.*

In language there are only differences.

Ferdinand de Saussure, *Course in General Linguistics.*

Semiotics is the science of signs. Its most distinctive theoretical characteristic is the negation of the division of subject from object which is the keystone of traditional Western science. Semiotics locates the sign, which it treats as an original unification of subject and object, in place of the old subject-object split at the center of scientific investigation. In Charles Sanders Peirce's original formulation, a sign represents something to someone. I have suggested that tourist attractions are signs…Sightseers do not, in any empirical sense, see San Francisco. They see Fisherman's Wharf, a cable car, the Golden Gate Bridge, Union Square, Coit Tower, the Presidio, City Lights Bookstore, Chinatown, and perhaps the Haight Ashbury or a nude go-go dancer in a North Beach-Barbary Coast club.

Dean MacCannell, *The Tourist: A New Theory of the Leisure Class.*

Chapter 2

Making a Semiotic Analysis of Tourist Icons

"This company is about icons." That's the way Patricio de Marco, the chief executive officer of Gucci, described the brand (quoted in Christina Passarillo, "Gucci Unpacks 'La Dolce Vita'"; *Wall Street Journal*, September 22, 2010, B1, B5). And spokespeople for most of the upscale brands would say the same thing about the brands they work for. What they mean by describing their brands as icons is that their brands are distinctive and known for being beautifully designed, well made and expensive. Gucci products can be identified by the Gucci logo—a mark that distinguishes Gucci products from other brands of products with which it competes. We can think of the various tourist sites I will be discussing in this book as being like "brands" that are competing with other iconic sites for visits by tourists.

Semiotics and Icons

The term "icon" has many meanings. It is used by semioticians to stand for something that generates meaning by resemblance. Semiotics can be described as the science of signs—a sign being anything that can be used to stand for something else. A word is a sign; thus the word "tree" stands for a large leafy plant, and a pine tree is a specific kind of tree. One of the founding fathers of semiotics, the philosopher C. S. Peirce, wrote:

> Every sign is determined by its object, either first, by partaking in the characters of the object, when I call a sign an *Icon*; secondly, by being really and in its individual existence connected with the individual object, when I call the sign an *Index*; Thirdly, by more or less certainty that it will be interpreted as denoting the object, in consequence of a habit (which term I use as including a natural disposition), when I call the sign a *Symbol*.(1977:36)

The term "icon" has been modified in popular usage in recent years and now stands for some kind of exemplary and culturally significant place or thing. And in some cases, we use the term "icon" to refer to a person—a famous politician or artist/performer. Technically, the word icon comes from the Greek *eikôn* which means image or likeness.

When I was in high school, one of my teachers called me an "iconoclast," which means, literally speaking, a breaker of icons and idols. That is, a non-conformist. In a sense, much of my career as a scholar and writer has involved "smashing" idols and icons in the sense of deconstructing their hidden meanings and considering their psychological, sociological, political, and cultural impacts. The discipline that uses these approaches is known as cultural studies—a kind of research that uses semiotics and concepts from a variety of disciplines—but most importantly semiotics, I suggest—to understand the significance of whatever is being investigated.

In this book I will be interpreting the meanings and cultural significance of a number of globally important iconic places and buildings and using these icons for a discussion of topics related to their symbolic meaning and the role they play in tourism. One of the more outstanding examples of analyzing icons is found in Roland Barthes's books *Mythologies* and *The Eiffel Tower and Other Mythologies*. In these books he deals with iconic aspects of French culture, such as "The New Citroen," "Plastic," "The Iconography of the Abbé Pierre" and "The Eiffel Tower," and offers a semiotically informed Marxist interpretation of them.

Barthes named his book *Mythologies* because he found in all the topics he discussed hidden bourgeois or capitalist ideologies that he believed helped shape French culture and society. As he writes in the preface to the 1972 edition of the book (1972:9):

> This book has a double theoretical framework: on the one hand, an ideological critique bearing on the language of so-called mass culture; on the other, a first attempt to analyze semiologically the mechanics of language. I had just read Saussure and as a result acquired the conviction that by treating "collective representations" as sign-systems, one might hope to go further than the pious show of unmasking them and account *in detail* for the mystification that transforms petit-bourgeois culture into a universal nature.

He used the term semiology, which was the term for the science of signs that was popular until it was replaced by Peirce's term semiotics in recent years. Barthes wrote another book, on Japanese culture, titled *Empire of Signs,* that serves as a model for my analysis of the icons in this book.

In *Empire of Signs* Barthes discussed in the first chapter, "Faraway," his methodology. He writes (1982:4), "The author has never, in any sense, photographed Japan. Rather, he has done the opposite: Japan has starred him with any number of 'flashes.'" By this he means that he will discuss certain aspects of Japan that struck him as significant and worth analyzing, but will not be offering a historical analysis or one based on conventional scholarship. For example, he has chapters on topics such as the "emptiness" in the center of Tokyo, the importance of train and subway stations, and spatial organization in Japan. All of these topics, and others that he deals with, can be seen, semiotically speaking, as signs, and it is the task of the semiotician to help explicate how these signs function and what they reveal. The thinker who provided the theories that shaped Barthes's thinking was Ferdiand de Saussure, the other founder of the science of signs, who used the term "semiology" (literally "words about signs").

In his book *Course in General Linguistics,* Saussure explains the basis of his theory. He writes (1915/1966:16):

> Language is a system of signs that express ideas, and is therefore comparable to a system of writing, the alphabet of deaf-mutes, symbolic rites, polite formulas, military signals, etc. But it is the most important of all these systems.
>
> *A science that studies the life of signs within society* is conceivable; it would be a part of social psychology and consequently of general psychology; I shall call it *semiology* (from Greek *sēmeîon* "sign"). Semiology would show what constitutes signs, what laws govern them. Since the science does not yet exist, no one can say what it would be; but it has a right to existence, a place staked out in advance.

From a semiotic perspective, the various iconic buildings and places that I'll be analyzing are all complex signs. That point was made by MacCannell, whom I quoted at the beginning of this chapter, in his influential book *The Tourist.* Saussure suggested that signs are made of two parts: a sound-object that he called a *signifier*, and a concept generated by the signifier called a *signified.* The relation that exists between a signifier and signified is culturally determined, not natural, which results in the fact that the meaning of signs can change over time.

A contemporary semiotician, Mark Gottdiener, offers us another perspective on the significance of signs. He writes in *The Theming of America: Dreams, Visions and Commercial Spaces* (1996:8–9):

The basic unit of semiotics is the *sign* defined conceptually as something that stands for something else, and, more technically, as a spoken or written word, a drawn figure, or a material object unified in the mind with a particular cultural concept. The sign is this unity of word-object, known as a *signifier* with a corresponding, culturally prescribed content or meaning, known as a *signified.* Thus our minds attach the word "dog," or the drawn figure of a "dog," as a signifier to the idea of a "dog," that is, a domesticated canine species possessing certain behavioral characteristics. If we came from a culture that did not possess dogs in daily life, however unlikely, we would not know what the signifier "dog" means. ... When dealing with objects that are signifiers of certain concepts, cultural meanings, or ideologies of belief, we can consider them not only as "signs," but *sign vehicles.* Signifying objects carry meanings with them.

The sign, something that stands for something else, is the basic concept in semiotics—the science of signs. The term *sēmeîon*, which is at the root of semiotics, means "sign." The buildings and sites that I will be discussing are signs, but they are also, in Gottdiener's perspective, sign vehicles that carry many meanings.

Saussure made another point that is important here. The meaning of concepts is relational; they don't have any meaning in themselves, and the basic relationship among signs is opposition. As he explained (1915/1966:117–118), "Concepts are purely differential and defined not by their positive content but negatively by their relations with the other terms of the system." It is not "content" that determines meaning, but "relations" that exist in some kind of a system. The "most precise characteristic" of these concepts, he adds, "is in being what the others are not.... Signs function, then, not through their intrinsic value but through their relative position." Saussure adds further (p. 123) that "in languages there are only differences," and we can use this concept to explore semiotic theory. It is differences that generate meaning, often found in oppositions such as rich and poor, weak and strong, beautiful and ugly. These insights inform the analyses of the global icons that I am to undertake.

As I explained earlier, semiotics, along with Marxist/ideological theory, psychoanalytic theory, sociological theory, historical research, and literary theory form a meta-discipline known as cultural studies. Cultural studies uses whatever theories it finds most relevant and appropriate— often in combinations such as semiotic/Marxist theory or sociological/

semiotic/psychoanalytic/Marxist theory—to analyze whatever topic is of interest to it, whether it be rock music or the Eiffel Tower. But, I would suggest, it is semiotics that is the "lead" discipline in cultural studies, and thus this book is informed primarily by semiotic analysis.

Metaphor and Metonymy

There are a number of other concepts that semioticians use when making their analysis. One of the most important is the difference between metaphor and metonymy. Metaphor communicates or conveys information by *analogy*: something that is not known is like, in certain ways, something that is known. Metonymy communicates or conveys information by *association*. When you think of X, it is connected, in your mind, to Y.

What we have to recognize is that metaphor plays an important role in our thinking. As George Lakoff and Mark Johnson explain in *Metaphors We Live By* (1980:3):

> Metaphor is typically viewed as a characteristic of language alone, a matter of words rather than thought or action. For this reason, most people think they can get along perfectly well without metaphor. We have found, on the contrary, that metaphor is pervasive in everyday life, not just in language but in thought and action. Our ordinary conceptual system, in terms of which we both think and act, is fundamentally metaphoric in nature.
>
> The concepts that govern our thought are not just matters of the intellect. They also govern our everyday functioning, down to the most mundane details. Our concepts structure what we perceive, how we get around in the world, and how we relate to other people. Our conceptual system thus plays a central role in defining our everyday realities.

We distinguish between metaphor and a weaker form of association called simile. In metaphor we use the word "is" in phrases such as "the mind is a machine." In simile we use the word "like" in phrases such as "the mind is like a machine." For example, we can analyze buildings in terms of things they are like. Thus, the Washington Monument, built to honor the father of our country, can be seen as a phallic symbol—a building that, in terms of its design, looks like a gigantic penis sticking up into the sky.

We can understand this if we recognize the role symbols play in our dreams and everyday lives. Sigmund Freud explains how phallic symbols work in his discussion of symbolism in dreams in his *A General Introduction to Psychoanalysis*. He writes: "The male genital organ is symbolically represented in dreams in many different ways, with most of which the common idea underlying the comparison is easily apparent… the penis is symbolically primarily by objects which resemble it in form, being long and upstanding. 1953:161." A building with a shape that is long and upstanding, such as the Washington Monument, can be seen, then, as being a phallic symbol—even if the architect who designed it didn't recognize this aspect of the building's design. Psychoanalytic theory assumes that people are never aware of the full significance of what they think, say, and do. The fact that the building honors the "father" of our country gives added weight to my description of the building as having a phallic quality. The closest womb symbol to the Washington Monument in Washington, D.C., would be the Lincoln Monument or possibly the Viet Nam Memorial.

There is a weak form of metonymy called synecdoche, in which a part is used to represent the whole and the whole is used to represent a part. When we say "The White House," we are using synecdoche to stand for the presidency, and when we say "The Pentagon," we are using that building to stand for the American military establishment.

Lakoff and Johnson offer us an interesting insight into the way metaphor and metonymy work. They write:

> Metaphor and metonymy are different kinds of processes. Metaphor is principally a way of conceiving of one thing in terms of another, and the primary function is understanding. Metonymy, on the other hand, has primarily a referential function that allows us to use one entity to stand for another. But metonymy is not merely a referential device. It also serves the function of providing understanding. (1980:36)

What is important to recognize is that metaphor and metonymy shape our thinking, and that it is quite common to find these devices in advertising, in architecture, and in many other aspects of life. A famous Chinese stadium, built for the 2008 Olympics, is known as the "Bird's Nest," because its design calls to mind a bird's nest. The process in calling the stadium a "Bird's Nest" is a simile. We are saying it is *like* a bird's nest. Our thinking, then, is dominated by analogies (metaphors) and associations (metonymies) we continually make in the course of every day.

Denotation and Connotation

In semiotic theory, we make a distinction between *denotation*, the tangible attributes of a building, and *connotation*, the cultural notions and matters tied to it. Thus, the denotative aspects of the Pentagon involve when it was built, how large it is, how many offices it contains, and other physical attributes of the building. The connotations connected with the Pentagon have to do with its role as the center of the American military services, its role in what has been described as the "Military-Industrial Complex" in the United States, its connection with military heroism, and its victimhood suffered when a plane controlled by Islamic terrorists crashed into it, killing many people.

When dealing with cultural icons, we may say that denotation is descriptive and tied to the physical attributes of the icon, while connotation is cultural and psychological, based on the various cultural meanings connected to the icon. Thus, for example, the Beijing National Stadium, also known as the "Bird's Nest" stadium, can be described, from a denotational point of view, as having a certain length and height and containing certain materials and taking a certain amount of money (US$423 million) and time (five years) to build. On the connotational level, the "Bird's Nest" stadium ties into our view of China and its economic and political power, and its relation to Chinese culture (a nation of master builders).

Semiotics, I suggest, offers us an important tool for finding meaning in everyday life and, for our purposes, in the cultural icons I will be analyzing. As the discussion of phallic symbols demonstrates, semiotic theory allied with psychoanalytic theory—and, as we shall see—with other theories, provides an important methodology for understanding and analyzing the cultural, social, and political significance of the icons I deal with in this book.

Theorizing Tourism: Analyzing Iconic Destinations by Arthur Asa Berger, 42–49.

The Taj Mahal, an immense mausoleum of white marble, built in Agra between 1631 and 1648 by order of the Mughal Emperor Shah Jahan, is the jewel of Muslim art in India and one of the universally admired masterpieces of the world's heritage. It no doubt partially owes its renown to the moving circumstances of its construction. Shah Jahan, in order to perpetuate the memory of his favourite wife, Mumtaz Mahal, who died in 1631, had this funerary mosque built. The monument, begun in 1632, was finished in 1648; unverified but nonetheless, tenacious, legends attribute its construction to an international team of several thousands of masons, marble workers, mosaicists and decorators working under the orders of the architect of the emperor, Ustad Ahmad Lahori.

Situated on the right bank of the Yamuna in a vast Mogul garden of some 17 ha, this funerary monument, bounded by four isolated minarets, reigns with its octagonal structure capped by a bulbous dome through the criss-cross of open perspectives offered by alleys or basins of water. The rigour of a perfect elevation of astonishing graphic purity is disguised and almost contradicted by the scintillation of a fairy-like decor where the white marble, the main building material, brings out and scintillates the floral arabesques, the decorative bands, and the calligraphic inscriptions which are incrusted in polychromatic pietra dura. The materials were brought in from all over India and central Asia and white Makrana marble from Jodhpur. Precious stones for the inlay came from Baghdad, Punjab, Egypt, Russia, Golconda, China, Afghanistan, Ceylon, Indian Ocean and Persia. The unique Mughal style combines elements and styles of Persian, Central Asian and Islamic architecture.

whc.unesco.org/en/list/252

Let the splendor of the diamond, pearl and ruby vanish like the magic shimmer of the rainbow. Only let this one teardrop, the Taj Mahal, glisten spotlessly bright on the cheek of time...

Rabindranath Tagore

Chapter 3

The Taj Mahal, Agra

The Taj Mahal, in Agra, is certainly one of India's most important iconic buildings and tourist sites, if not its most famous one. It also is one of the most famous buildings in the world. Shortly after returning from India, I attended a party and got into a conversation about our trip with a woman who had been to India a number of years ago. "I only went to India," she said, "because I wanted to see the Taj Mahal. I remember when I first saw it. I stood mesmerized by it, unable to take my eyes off it, almost hypnotized by its unbelievable beauty." We can contrast this "romantic" description of the building's significance with the description of a friend, a former editor of mine, who told me he had been to India and seen the Taj Mahal. "What did you think of it?" I asked. "It's a big white building," he replied.

These descriptions reflect polar oppositions relative to the beauty of the Taj Mahal. The woman's description I would describe as romantic. As the result of reading various things about the Taj Mahal, she was programmed, one might say, to see the building as exquisite and thus was "hypnotized" by its beauty. My former editor, a more pragmatic person—but a sophisticated one with a degree from Harvard University—saw it from a denotative perspective. It is a big white building—though, of course, it is much more than that.

Going to see the Taj Mahal involves a number of steps. You drive to a parking lot, and there you take a vehicle that is battery operated for a five minute ride to the area where the Taj Mahal is located. When you buy your ticket to see the Taj Mahal, you are given a small bottle of water and plastic coverings for your shoes. Then you pass through a gate and finally get to see the Taj Mahal and other buildings that are part of the complex. The electric vehicles are used to prevent pollution from damaging the building. Our guide told us that all new manufacturing plants had been moved to the outskirts of Agra, to cut down on pollution and acid rain—but during the night I visited the Taj Mahal, I could hardly see it because of the pollution. My hotel was a kilometer away from it, and from my hotel's top floor, which had a viewing area, I could only see the Taj Mahal as a vague form due to the pollution.

The workmanship in the building is incredible, with remarkably delicate marble screens and other carvings, and many inlaid jewels. The Taj Mahal, most people would say, is a very beautiful building and a remarkable one, as well. What I wonder about the Taj Mahal is how much of the appeal of the building to tourists is due to "hype" generated by scores of writers and journalists, and the history connected with it, and how much is due to its intrinsic beauty? There are a number of aspects that contribute to the beauty of the building—and all buildings. What makes a building beautiful is controversial, but certain things seem important:

the design of a building, and the relationship between its various elements

the warmth conveyed by its elements

the setting of the building and its relation to its surroundings

the balance between the bulding's shape, color, and the textures of the material used in it

the way the light affects it

Aesthetically speaking, the Taj Mahal strikes most people as masterful architectural achievement. The workmanship on the outside and inside of the building is quite remarkable. Second, we must consider its setting. It is set in a large garden area, with a huge rectangular pool that reflects it. We can say that the Taj Mahal's relationship to its surroundings is very satisfying. The combination of the design of the building, the workmanship shown in the building, and its setting helps generate the powerful impact the building has on most people.

In his book *The Tourist*, Dean MacCannell discusses "markers," which he defines as "information about a specific sight" (1976:110). Generally speaking, before tourists visit an iconic place, like the Taj Mahal, they will have read about it in articles, seen it in travel literature, and have learned something about it in other markers. I would suggest that these markers play a role in the way tourists see sites and react to them. Tourists have been, in a sense, conditioned by markers to have certain responses.

There are many other very beautiful buildings in India, and in other countries as well, but few have the aura, the cultural resonance, of the Taj Mahal and the capacity to generate the kinds of feelings found in many who visit it. As the authors of the *Lonely Planet India* write (2005:357), "As an architectural masterpiece, it stands head and shoulders above any other contenders."

The history or back story of the building contributes to its mystique. It was built as a memorial by Emperor Shah Jahan for his second (some historians say third) wife, Mumtaz Mahal, who died in 1631 giving birth to their fourteenth child. Shah Jahan was the grandson of the emperor Akbar. According to the legend, Sha Jahan was so distraught by the death of Mumtaz that his hair turned white overnight. He started building the mausoleum in 1631 and finished it in 1653. So it took more than twenty years to build and required 20,000 workers to complete it, at a cost, in today's money, of around 70 million dollars. The Taj Mahal is also part of a love story, and this matter of losing a loved one and creating a monument in response to this loss makes it, semiotically speaking, a signifier of the power of love and remembrance that has the capacity to help evoke emotions in most people who visit the building.

The Taj Mahal is built on a raised marble platform, which means when you see the Taj Mahal, it is always seen silhouetted against the sky. When the sun is out and the sky is blue, the white marble of the Taj Mahal glistens radiantly. Four minarets are on the corners of the area where the building is located. One is leaning slightly, which our guide said was God's way of showing human fallibility. The dramatic setting of the building helps contribute to its emotional impact on visitors.

An important part of the appeal of travel is what can be described as "time travel," which involves—metaphorically—going back to earlier times to see the wonders of the world. The Taj Mahal, finished in 1651, enables us to get a glimpse of what earlier architects were capable of doing, to walk where once emperors and kings did, and to gaze upon the fruits of Shah Jahan's love. We can say, adopting a uses and gratifications approach, that it provides tourists with an opportunity to participate in history and to see an authentic architectural treasure—the most outstanding example of Mughal (that is, Muslim) architecture. I already discussed the importance of the concept of "authenticity" in tourism studies and suggested that for many contemporary tourists, authenticity is not important. And yet it seems obvious that it is the authenticity of the building, the fact that they are actually seeing *the* Taj Mahal, the *real* Taj Mahal, along with its beauty, that draws so many tourists to go to Agra, an otherwise unimpressive city.

Tourists who come to Agra to see the Taj Mahal are generally heritage cultural tourists, who are interested in seeing, for themselves, some of the great artistic achievements of mankind—what the UNESCO World Heritage site describes as "masterpieces of human creative genius." Because of the anxiety most people in the West have about visiting India, generally involving health issues, it is reasonable to assume that most of the tourists who come to India do so as part of organized tours and are, in Cohen's theory, either organized mass tourists or individual mass tourists.

There is an ironic twist to the love story behind the building of the Taj Mahal. It turns out that one of Shah Jahan's sons, Aurangzeb, overthrew his father in 1658 and imprisoned him in the Agra Fort, so Shah Jahan spent his remaining years in a fort where he could look out over the Yamuna River and see his beloved Taj Mahal, glistening in the sun. Shah Jahan gained his throne, so I've read, by killing some of his brothers, so his fate can be said to be doubly ironic. According to our guide, Aurangzeb imprisoned Shah Jahan because he was planning to build another Taj Mahal, in black marble, on the other size of the Yamuna River, and Aurangzeb feared this would bankrupt the city. From a psychoanalytic perspective, we can say that there probably was an element of the Oedipal Complex at work here—the Oedipus myth, Freud pointed out, involves conflicts between sons and their fathers. Whatever the case, the Taj Mahal stands as a monument signifying Shah Jahan's love and as a universally recognized triumph of Mughal architecture.

Theorizing Tourism: Analyzing Iconic Destinations by Arthur Asa Berger, 50–55.

In the fall of 1928, an eager young actor was introduced at a New York movie house to rave reviews. He wasn't very handsome, with protruding ears like Bing Crosby, and a wider mouth than Martha Ray. His voice was high-pitched, yes squeaky. But, of even more significance, he was not even human, but belonged to the rodent family.

Michael Brody, "The Wonderful World of Disney—Its Psychological Appeal"

Disneyland is a perfect model of all the entangled orders of simulacra. It is first of all a play of illusions and phantasms: the Pirates, the Frontier, the Future World, etc. This imaginary world is supposed to ensure the success of the operation. But what attracts the crowds most is without doubt the social microcosm, the religious, miniaturized pleasure of real America, of its constraints and joys. One parks outside and stands in line inside, one is altogether abandoned at the exit. The only phantasmagoria in this imaginary world lies in the tenderness and warmth of the crowd, and in the sufficient and excessive number of gadgets necessary to create the multitudinous effect. The contrast with the absolute solitude of the parking lot—a veritable concentration camp—is total.

Jean Baudrillard, *The Precession of Simulacra*

Chapter 4

Disneyland, California

Walt Disney offered the following comments when Disneyland, his theme park, named for himself, opened on July 17, 1955:

> To all who come to this happy place, welcome. Disneyland is your land. Here age relives fond memories of the past...and here youth may savor the challenge and promise of the future. Disneyland is dedicated to the ideals, the dreams, and the hard facts that have created America...with the hope that it will be a source of joy and inspiration to all the world.

This was the beginning of a theme park empire that has Disneylands in many different countries and a media giant whose films and stores are found all over the world. The Disney phenomenon has attracted the attention of scholars from many disciplines and is the subject of many debates as to the significance of Disneyland and the other Disney creations.

In Richard Schickel's *The Disney Version* (1968:95) Disney describes how he created Mickey Mouse:

> His head was a circle with an oblong circle for a snout. The ears were also circles so they could be drawn the same no matter how he turned his head.
>
> His body was like a pear and he had a long tail. His legs were pipestems and we stuck them in big shoes [also circular] to give him the look of a kid wearing his father's shoes.
>
> We didn't want him to have mouse hands, because he was supposed to be more human. So we gave him gloves. Five fingers looked like too much on such a little figure, so we took one away. That was just one less finger to animate.
>
> To provide a little detail, we gave him the two-button pants. There was no mouse hair or any other frills that would slow down animation.

We can see in this statement Disney's desire to subordinate the creative process to the demands of technology. It was the need to be able to crank out Mickey Mouse images quickly that determined the way he looks. Disney was obliged to produce 700 feet of film every two weeks and needed a figure that was easy to draw. This attention to detail and control was to shape his films and later his theme parks. Disney had taken his children to amusement parts and was disturbed by how dirty and tawdry they were. His innovation was to create a theme park, based on his characters, that was clean and wholesome.

Jan Morris, one of the best travel writers of our times, found herself feeling "uneasy" in Los Angeles and in Disneyland. As she explained in her article "Los Angeles: The Know-How City," originally published in *Rolling Stone* in 1976 and republished in her book *Destinations: Essays from Rolling Stone* (1982:98):

> For myself, I am left with an uneasy feeling, even about Disneyland, where the most advanced technical resources, the most brilliant administrative systems, are used simply to animate a gigantic charade. The sham treads uncomfortably upon the heels of truth, and one begins to wonder whether a dummy castle from Snow White, a make-believe New Orleans restaurant, even a nonalcoholic mint julep might not be as good, and as true, as the real thing. I found this inescapable illusion rather suffocating, and was revived, as I staggered from the King Arthur Carousel to the Casey Jr. Circus Train, through Tomorrowland to the Bear Country, only by the presence of the peripatetic bands, blues, brass, or Mexican, who really were undeniably alive and irreplaceable by electronics even in L.A.

One reason Morris is such a great travel writer is that her feelings about the places she visits are so perceptive and interesting and her use of the English language is so superb. The adjectives with which she describes Disneyland, "uneasy" and "suffocating," offer us an insight into the ambience of Disneyland and its impact that is at odds with the way it describes itself.

Disneyland advertises itself as "the happiest place on earth," but is it? In an article by a psychiatrist, Michael Brody, "The Wonderful World of Disney," we get a different picture. In the first part of his essay he deals with anal themes in Disney's cartoons and other work and quotes Richard Schickel, who described Disney in *The Disney Version* as follows: "There was always something obsessive about Walt Disney's personality. There was his parsimony, his single-minded concentration, and his need for order and details" (1976:350).

This description of Disney's personality is very similar to Sigmund Freud's description of anal erotics (in *Freud: Character and Culture*, edited by Philip Rieff): "The persons I am about to describe are remarkable for a regular combination of the three following peculiarities: they are exceptionally *orderly, parsimonious,* and *obstinate*" (1963:27)

There are good reasons, then, to suggest that Walt Disney had elements of anal eroticism in his personality and that his psychological makeup was to be reflected in his films and in Disneyland, the only theme park that he personally created.

Brody then discusses Disneyland (1975:350):

Here, in "his" magic kingdom he would come after nightfall to pick up litter missed by his army of sanitation workers. Disney strove for control over his work and destiny. What could be more natural than a huge, controlled playground, where all could be Disney-regulated.

There is excellent crowd control here. We are led on by the next attraction up the street. Lines may be long, but broken up into smaller units, they appear shorter.

Employees are young and clean-cut. All go to a training school for smile and behavior regulation.

Most of the attractions are computerized, with their stars an agent's dream, well-controlled examples of yet another Disney marvel: audio-animatronics....The overall park environment couldn't be cleaner...even the lakes, forests and beaches are ecologically planned. Waste baskets blend with the scenery and there is even a crew of chewing gum scrapers. "Dirty" money is exchanged for clean, fresh colorful coupons.

As a result of all this regulation and compartmentalization, Brody explains, you also find passivity. People who attend the park have little to do except become receptacles of experiences. "Except for a penny arcade," he writes, "there are no skills to be tested or games to be played" (1975: 8).

The folksy "Uncle Walter" exterior, the genial and amiable "Walt," was a mask for a person driven by powerful forces that helped shape his great creation, Disneyland, where everyone could be subtly controlled and their behavior regulated. Naming the park after himself also suggests an element of narcissism and maybe even grandiosity. One question we may ask is this—does the popularity of Disneyland, with its anal themes, signify the same psychological attributes of the people who go there, or is Disneyland a kind of momentary vacation from freedom to enjoy the pleasures of structure and control?

Many scholars have found interesting things to say about Disneyland, Disney World, and the whole Disney phenomenon. Socio-semiotician

Mark Gottdiener offers some important insights in a paper, "Disneyland: A Utopian Urban Space." He discusses a topic Brody mentioned, the matter of social control and writes:

> In Disneyland social control is refined to an art, the art of moving crowds by their own motivation instead of coercion. D-land represents the ideal in this regard. It is the perfection of subordination: people digging their own fantasy graves. Los Angeles, in contrast, is the site of the coercive mechanisms of wage labor, ideology, and state power. This space also controls by the separation and isolation of people. (1982:139)

He compares the kind of subtle social control found in Disneyland with Los Angeles, where real-world considerations are the mechanisms of social control.

Then he moves on to another topic, namely the "illusion" people attending Disneyland have about its costs and the way the cost of entering Disneyland acts as a filter mechanism, screening out undesirable people, in terms of their socio-economic status. Disneyland thus becomes a classless, because all middle-class, micro-society. He writes:

> Disneyland presents the illusion of cornucopia. After paying a lump sum at the entrance to the park, participants enjoy an abundance of opportunity for amusement. Prior to the 1980s rides were portioned out by varied individual prices, some of which were relatively expensive. Since July 1981 the lump sum payment, which is over $20 a person, now allows visitors to unlimited access to all rides—a true cornucopia, if you can afford the entrance fee.
>
> In the theme park space, class distinctions are minimized and ignored, because the poor have been screened out of the park by the price of admission. In this world, corporate control is benevolent and even paternal. A ride is "brought to you by," "with the compliments of," and "presented by." These epithets are unobtrusive and subliminal. They are extended in the manner of a gift, therefore they invoke the traditional economy of a tribal society. The insidious implication here is that such courtesies are reciprocal. (1982:140)

Gottdiener wrote his article well before the price of a ticket to Disneyland became $91 for children three to nine and $101 for children ten and over and adults. There are numerous package deals available, but a visit to Disneyland is not cheap by any means.

4. *Disneyland, California*

Gottdiener next turns his attention to two interesting matters: first, that Disneyland can be considered a postmodern kind of entertainment, and second, that in Disneyland, there is a role reversal and children make the most important decisions.

> In Disneyland, the built environment is entertaining. Every edifice has symbolic value, much as was the case for ancient and medieval cities. Disneyland, as the most successful theme park, helped inaugurate the entertainment culture of postmodernism....
>
> Finally, Disneyland inverts the structure of family authority. While most families, regardless of class, are adult-directed even if they are child-centered, a visit to D-land is ostensibly for children (or tourist visitors who then are ascribed the status of children). Here the child gets to direct the adults. Invariably they choose the rides, the food, and the schedule. Parents become chaperones or vicarious thrill seekers through the eyes of their own offspring. (1982:140)

This role that parents take in Disneyland seems to have spread beyond the confines of Disney's creations, and now, increasingly, young children are involved in decisions parents make about purchasing cars and other things.

Semiotically speaking, Disneyland has become a global signifier of American culture, and that is one of the reasons why it has attracted the attention of so many cultural theorists in America and elsewhere. Disneyland is, from a semiotic perspective, an example of synecdoche: a part that reflects the whole. It claims to be authentic with its recreation of various aspects of American life and society, but it is really a pseudo-America. Almost everything in Disneyland is fake. People come to Disneyland to be amused and entertained, to satisfy their curiosity about what it is like, and, in the case of families, to give their children what they hope will be a memorable experience. But as Gottdiener points out, what visitors to Disneyland get is control and cleverly disguised long lines for its attractions. Foreign tourists often visited Disneyland because of their curiosity about it, but now there are Disneylands in many countries, so going there isn't as big an attraction for visitors to America.

Sharon Zukin, in her book *Point of Purchase: How Shopping Changed American Culture,* suggests that Disneyland became the model for stores. She writes (2005:221): "Disneyland has shaped much of our thinking about the social spaces of stores. As a merchandising model, Disneyland suggests the advantages a store can draw from providing 'circuses'—

attractions besides the merchandise—in order to give shoppers a 'memorable experience.'" Disney has, in fact, created its own stores that sell its products, tying itself into its role as an archetype of American popular culture and trying, as Zukin puts it, to spread the Disney "aura" everywhere. It is possible that the Apple corporation used Disney's stores as a model to be imitated. The term "aura" suggests authenticity and was used by the cultural critic Walter Benjamin, who wrote in a famous essay, "The Work of Art in the Age of Mechanical Reproduction" (1974:615), that "the presence of the original is the prerequisite to the concept of authenticity" [in Mast and Cohen's *Film Theory and Practice,* 1974.] Modernist tourists seek authenticity, and postmodernist critics, as was discussed earlier, do not care about reality and authenticity. They just want to be entertained. This lack of authenticity in Disneyland may help explain the French sociologist Jean Baudrillard's postmodern analysis of the theme park.

Its cultural resonance may explain why he took so much interest in Disney and suggested that Disneyland is the reality and the United States is the simulation. As Baudrillard explained in an article "Disney World Company":

> Disney, the precursor, the grand initiator of the imaginary as virtual reality, is now in the process of capturing all the real world to integrate it into a synthetic universe, in the form of a vast "reality show," where reality itself becomes a spectacle, where the real becomes a theme park. (www.egs/edu/faculty/jean-baudrillard/articles/diisneyworld-company, March 4, 1996)

In his celebrated article "The Precision of Simulacra," Baudrillard expanded his analysis of Disneyland:

> Everywhere in Disneyland the objective profile of America, down to the morphology of individuals and of the crowd, is drawn. All its values are exalted by the miniature and the comic strip....Disneyland exists in order to hide that it is the "real" country, all of "real" America that *is* Disneyland....Disneyland is presented as imaginary in order to make us believe that the rest is real, whereas all of Los Angeles and the America that surrounds it are no longer real, but belong to the hyperreal order and to the order of simulation. (www.egs.ed/faculty/jean-baudrillard/articles/simulacra-and-simulations-i-the-precession-of-simulacra. February 15, 1995)

4. *Disneyland, California*

Disney himself was cryogenized and maybe, at some future date, if technology evolves the way Disney hopes it will, he will rise from the dead. When he thaws out, God only knows what else he will think up to further "entertain" Americans and tourists all over the world—and, as Marxist critics would say, temporarily enslave tourists in his semi-fascist entertainment fantasy lands.

Theorizing Tourism: Analyzing Iconic Destinations by Arthur Asa Berger, 56–63.
© 2013 Left Coast Press, Inc. All rights reserved.

The Paradise Paradox

Romantic Westerners once sold Balinese culture to the globe. Now locals wonder if their island is becoming a giant theme park.

BIG MACS in the macrobiotic hills of Ubud? West Bali National Park handed over to a timber magnate for eco-tourism? Similar rumors of development doom have been flying on Indonesia's fabled island ever since the 1930s, when it was first marketed to the world as paradise on earth. True or not, the latest whispers making the rounds point to an increasingly gnawing worry. More and more Balinese are asking: Is our home being turned into a giant theme park?

Nothing perhaps has stoked fears more that Bali is being Disneyfied than the 40-story (140-meter) statue of the mythical Garuda bird that sculptor I Nyoman Nuarta is creating across from the international airport. Once it is completed in a couple of years, you can be sure tourist brochures will describe it as "The Largest in the World!"

A recent history of Bali might well be called The Paradise Paradox. Here we have an Asian culture that was sold to the world by Western romantics, a Hindu island in a mostly Muslim archipelago, a tourist destination that is at once commercial and deeply spiritual. While other famous tropical idylls have succumbed to jet-loads of fun-seekers, Bali culture has proved itself remarkably resilient. Nor have the people utterly lost out to the powerful business elites from the neighboring island of Java. Nonetheless, with the government planning to divide the island into 21 tourist zones, locals and tourists alike are wondering yet again whether Bali's photogenic dances and festivals, beaches and rice terraces can survive intact.

Keith Loveard, "The Paradise Paradox"

64

Bali: An Exotic Disneyland

As I read through the travel guides to Bali, which are often very clear about the commercialization of Balinese culture and the problems that tourism has created for Bali, I couldn't help but wonder about Loveard's hypothesis—is Bali becoming a Southeast Asian Disneyland? Disneyland advertises itself as a paradise, as "The Happiest Place on Earth." Bali is conventionally seen as a "tropical island Paradise," but one that has made many accommodations to suit the needs of its highly developed tourism industry. Let me suggest some comparisons and differences between Disneyland (and Disney World) and Bali.

Disneyland/World	Bali
Man-Made Paradise	Natural Paradise
Artificial	Semi-Artificial
Hyper-Clean Aseptic	Messy, Dirty
Pop Culture Rituals	Ethnographic Culture Rituals
Contrived Spectacles	Religious Spectacles
Disney Corporation	Indonesian Tourism Officials

Disneyland, the self-proclaimed "Happiest Place on Earth," is a contrived paradise, a theme-park that is obsessively clean and one in which Disney's pop culture characters, such as Mickey Mouse, hold sway. Workers in Disneyland are trained to smile and taught how to relate to patrons, who generally pay a considerable amount of money to go to Disneyland. The executives in the Disney corporation who created and run Disneyland and Disney World pay a great deal of attention to how they are perceived by people who visit them, and have a vested interest in making certain, to the extent they can, that visitors come back.

An America scholar, S. M. Fjellman, explains the degrees of fakery found in Disney as follows: "The concepts of real and fake, however, are too blunt to capture the subtlety of Disney simulations. As WDW things are not just real or fake but real real, fake real, real fake, and fake fake" (1992:253). The Disney theme parks thus pose a problem to scholars who try to make sense of them. There are so many different kinds of simulations that it is hard to grasp what is happening in these parks.

This question of authenticity in Disneyland and Disney World has relevance for our understanding of tourism in Bali. Bali is, of course, far different from the Disney creations in that Bali is an island with a distinctive culture—but one that has evolved in many respects, scholars tell us, to meet the requirements of tourists who visit the island. The influx of tourism in Bali has been produced, in part, by the Indonesian government, which decided to make Bali into a major tourism destination—because of the money to be gained by doing so. The Indonesian government also wanted to protect Bali's distinctive culture, to the extent they could, from the "ravages" of mass tourism. There is considerable question about the extent to which Bali's culture (or any culture "penetrated" by mass tourism) has been affected, for better or worse, by this phenomenon. Michel Picard's suggestion seems reasonable: we can't know whether tourism's influence is good or bad in Bali, so we should focus our attention on how the Balinese have responded to tourism, moving from what he describes as cultural tourism to a touristic culture.

Michel Picard is a French anthropologist and the author of one of the most important books on Bali, *Bali: Cultural Tourism and Touristic Culture* (1996). Picard also discusses the question of Bali's "Disneyfication" and the impact that tourism is having on the island. He writes, in an essay titled "Creating a New Version of Paradise," that:

> The Island of Bali has long been characterized in the West as the last "paradise" on earth—a traditional society insulated from the modern world and its vicissitudes, whose inhabitants are endowed with exceptional artistic talents and consecrate a considerable amount of time and wealth staging sumptuous ceremonies for their own pleasure and that of their gods—now also for the delectation of foreign visitors.
>
> This image is due in large part of course to the positive effects Bali's manifold charms have on visitors, but we should recognize that it is also the result of certain romantic Western notions about what constitutes a "tropical island paradise" in the first place. Moreover, we need to understand that Bali's development into a popular tourist destination has been the result of specific actions on the part of governing authorities. (1999:82)

This quote offers a capsule view of his analysis of Balinese tourism. Picard argues that we should not ask whether the impact of tourism on Bali (or anyplace, for that matter) is positive or negative but should look at how tourism impacts on Bali and how the Balinese have responded to tourism. What we find in Bali is similar to what we find in another "paradise," Luang Prabang, in Laos—in both places the national government played a major role in the their development as tourist destinations.

A Note on the Exotic

Tourists are in search of differences; that's one of the reasons they travel. Cultural tourists come to Bali because of its rich and remarkable culture, as reflected in its wonderful dances and its music, and beach tourists come to enjoy its lovely beaches. Tourists want to eat different kinds of foods, to see different sites, and to experience different cultures. The term that best characterizes cultures that are most different from Western European ones is "the exotic." We can characterize the exotic by contrasting it with its opposite, the ordinary or everyday. We can see the difference between these two concepts in the chart that follows. This chart shows that there are many different areas in which the exotic differs from the everyday and helps explain the appeal of the exotic to the imagination of the tourist. French culture, for example, may be considerably different from American culture, but French culture is not exotic, while Balinese culture is.

EVERYDAY LIFE	THE EXOTIC
Near	Distant
The Present	The Past
Familiar	Strange
Modern	Ancient, Traditional
The Skyscraper	The Hut
The Supermarket	The Souk
Cathedrals	Hindu Temples, Mosques
Euro-American Cuisine	Ethnic Cuisines
Electronic	Mechanical
Suits, Dresses	Turbans, Robes, Costumes

Western tourists search for the exotic because it provides them with that which is most different from their way of life and provides them with one of the more important gratifications that tourists seek—first hand insights into the way people in other countries live. Visits to exotic tourist destinations allow people to gain a sense of fellowship with mankind, and, in the case of Bali, to see beautiful places and see or participate in the numerous religious rituals there. Hardly a day goes by in Ubud, Bali's most important cultural tourism destination, where there isn't a religious parade or some kind of a religious event. Many years ago, Bali primarily attracted adventurers and what Plog would call allocentric tourists. Now, with its well developed tourism facilities, it attracts psychocentric tourists, who want to experience the exotic, but in a place where they will feel safe, and for some, where they can feel comfortable in a tourist bubble in an expensive hotel or resort.

Cultural Tourism and Touristic Cultures

Cultural tourism refers, here, to the policy adopted by the Dutch rulers of Bali, and later by the Indonesian government when Indonesia had gained independence, to make Bali into an important tourist destination. This has been spectacularly (a word chosen on purpose) successful, as tourism in Bali went from 6,000 visitors in 1969 to approximately 10 million visitors in 2010. In a review of Picard's book, Shinji Yamashita, one of the foremost scholars of tourism in Bali (and author of *Bali and Beyond: Explorations in the Anthropology of Tourism,* which was discussed earlier), suggests that tourism has now become an increasingly important aspect of the study of culture nowadays and that in many places "traditional dress, traditional houses, and traditional dances exist only for tourists."

Yamashita goes on to explain that the Balinese decided to focus on, as one of their slogans put it, "Tourism for Bali, not Bali for tourism." It is as a result of becoming conscious of the importance of their culture, financially and otherwise, that the Balinese decided to "stage" their culture for tourists and become a "touristic culture." This has reached the point, Picard argues, that it is now impossible, in many cases, to differentiate between arts that were "ethnographic" or, in other words, historically authentic, and arts that are created or staged for tourists.

New Understandings of Culture

This transition in tourism, Yamashita argues, has changed the way we see culture—as dynamic and not static, especially as culture relates to tourism. As he writes:

> Culture now exists as a hybrid entity which is consciously manipulated, reconstructed and consumed. It will also be increasingly difficult in future [*sic*] to use the old-fashioned ethnographic methodology of describing a single culture by simplifying and adjusting it to fit the standard pattern of a particular region and people as an isolated island within society.... Within this context, tourism is becoming a crucial subject for study— along with others such as the issues of economic development, AIDS, gender, the media, and ethnic conflicts. (2003:4)

Tourism has led, then, to a major change in the way we think about culture. Anthropologists used to think of the "traditional" that they investigated as essentially static and unchanging, or as "authentic." Now, thanks to our focus on tourism as a part of anthropology, we see cultures as dynamic, always changing, always evolving. And often being changed by tourism.

Cultures, according to this definition of the term, are not "dead" specimens examined in the moral equivalent of a Petri dish by anthropologists who were "parachuted" down into the middle of isolated "primitive" and supposedly static cultures. Cultures are, and have always been, evolving and changing, even if we didn't recognize that this was so. I should point out that there are an estimated 100 different definitions of culture that have been offered by anthropologists and scholars in other disciplines. What follows is a definition from the *Dictionary of Sociology and Related Terms* that I like because it covers most of the ideas associated with the concept of culture:

> A collective name for all behavior patterns socially acquired and transmitted by means of symbols, hence a name for the distinctive achievements of human groups, including not only such items as language, tool-making, industry, art, science, law, government, morals and religion, but also the material instruments or artifacts in which cultural achievements are embodied and by which intellectual cultural features are given practical effect, such as buildings, tools, machines, communication devices, art objects.... As culture is transmitted by processes of teaching and learning, whether formal or informal, by what is called "inter-learning," the essential part of culture is to be found in patterns embodied in social traditions of the group, that is, the knowledge, ideas, values, standards and sentiments prevalent in the group. (Fairchild, 1967:80)

Clifford Geertz devotes a considerable amount of attention to under-standings of what culture is and how it is to be studied in his book *The Interpretation of Cultures.* He writes (1973:5): "The concept of culture I espouse and whose utility the essays below attempt to demonstrate, is essentially a semiotic one." Geertz has a number of chapters in his book on Bali, which he describes as having (1973:170) "perhaps the most rich-ly stocked lumber-room of gracious and magical beliefs and practices in Southeast Asia." His use of the term "interpretation" in his title suggests that dealing with culture is, to a great extent, a matter of interpretation and not simply a matter of data collection. After all, after data are col-lected, they still have to be interpreted.

One problem with Yamashita's hypothesis, his suggestion that cul-tures are always evolving, is that if cultures are always changing to suit the needs and desires of people in a particular culture (or tourists who come to visit that culture), is there anything we can call a culture? Or a distinctive culture? Are these changes in cultures leading to what Claude

Lévi-Strauss called a "monoculture," a world-wide culture that is essentially the same everywhere? There are reasons to question the monoculture hypothesis. If you think about individuals, they change all the time, yet most of the time they also maintain their identities and personalities. So change doesn't necessarily mean a loss of identity, or, in the case of Bali, a loss of "authentic" Balinese culture.

Can Paradises Change? Adam and Eve in the Garden of Eden

One reason we tend to think of primitive cultures as unchanging comes, I would suggest, from the most important paradise story for those living in the first world countries of the West—namely the story of Adam and Eve in the Garden of Eden. In that story, Adam and Eve exist in a natural paradise, the Garden of Eden. They can remain in the Garden for eternity, but one thing is forbidden to them—eating from the tree of the knowledge of good and evil. As we read in the Book of Genesis:

> And the Lord God planted a garden eastward in Eden; and there he put the man whom he had formed. And out of the ground made the Lord God to grow every tree that is pleasant to the sight, and good for food; the tree of life also in the midst of the garden, and the tree of knowledge of good and evil.

God told Adam, the first man, that if he ate from the tree of knowledge of good and evil he would die. But Eve, the first woman, was beguiled by the serpent that lived in the Garden and ate from the tree of knowledge of good and evil and also convinced Adam to eat from it. This led to "the Fall" ("In Adam's fall, we sinned all") and as a result of Adam's transgressions, Adam and Eve were thrown out of the Garden of Eden, he was condemned to work, women were condemned to bear their children "in sorrow" and the serpent was condemned to slither on its belly, with eternal enmity between serpents and human beings.

It is only after Adam's and Eve's eyes "were opened" that they recognized that they were naked, and so they sewed fig leaves together to hide their nakedness. And Adam and Eve and all human beings after them were no longer to have eternal life. We see this in the passage where God says to Adam, "For dust thou art, And unto dust shalt thou return."

The expulsion of Adam and Eve opens the door to human history, for before their expulsion, they lived in a kind of eternal present, without awareness of good and evil or almost anything else, for that matter. I would suggest that in the popular mind people see Paradise as static, as unchanging, as not influenced by good and evil and human transgressions. That is why, I believe, many people bring to Bali, and other so-called "tropical paradises," unreal expectations and a notion that people in Bali and other Southeast Asian paradises exist in a state of radical and unchanging innocence. A visit to Bali becomes, in a sense, a return to paradise before Adam's fall.

In this scenario, the tourist becomes the serpent, bringing not only knowledge of good and evil but actual good and evil to the Adamic innocents living in Bali and other "natural paradises" elsewhere. We can see interesting parallels between the Paradise story in the Bible and ideas and attitudes about tourism in Bali.

THE GARDEN	BALI
Adam and Eve	Balinese People
The Serpent	Tourists in Bali
Knowledge of Right and Wrong	Modernism and Postmodernism
Expulsion	Destruction of Balinese Culture

The problem with this comparison is that it assumes that Bali, like the Garden of Eden, is unchanging and that its inhabitants are unaware of the modern world and have not been affected by it.

Tourists who have naïve and unrealistic notions of what Bali is like are probably going to be shocked when they discover that Bali is highly commercialized and that the aspects of Balinese culture to which tourists are exposed have been shaped, in large measure, by both governmental bureaucrats in Indonesia and the Balinese people, in response to the perceived desires of visiting international tourists to Bali. There are numerous luxury hotels and resorts that cater to upscale visitors, whom I've described as "hierarchical elitists," and there are many tourism companies that provide package vacations at reasonable costs for mass tourists and individual tourists. There are also very expensive hotels for people who wish to avoid mass tourists.

Tourists in Bali can visit numerous temples and other culturally significant sites there, can spend time at Bali's markets, can attend Balinese traditional dance exhibitions, can spend time at Bali's wonderful beaches, and can explore, to the extent they wish, Bali's remarkable and rich culture.

5. *Bali: An Exotic Disneyland*

When we visited Bali a number of years ago, we stayed in a beautiful hotel in a lush, tropical garden for $25 a night. One of my doctors, a woman in her forties, recently got married. She told me, "We had our honeymoon in Bali in a beautiful resort. It's a marvelous place." And then she got an expression on her face as she thought about her visit there, an expression of absolute bliss, which made me think that Bali, even though it has many problems, still works its magic on tourists.

[Note: Parts of this chapter draw upon material in my book *Bali Tourism* (Routledge) in press.]

Theorizing Tourism: Analyzing Iconic Destinations by Arthur Asa Berger, 64–73.

Which brings us to the Rock Garden, Ryoanji's major claim to superstar status. It is a simple rock garden, consisting of nothing but white gravel/sand and 15 rocks, laid out just after the Onin Wars in the late 15th century. Put simply, this rock garden is acknowledged to be one of the absolute masterpieces of Japanese culture. The simple yet striking garden is just 30 meters long from east to west and 10 meters from north to south. There are no trees, just 15 irregularly shaped rocks of varying sizes, some surrounded by moss, arranged in a bed of white gravel/sand that is raked every day. The elimination of trees and plants and overall simplicity is reminiscent of abstract art. Conceptually it is as far from the ornate gardens of the contemporary court nobles in medieval feudal Japan as imaginable. It is sometimes hard to imagine that two such contrasting styles could emerge from the same 15th century culture. The garden is constructed in the "dry landscape" style called Karesansui. The rocks of various sizes are arranged on small white pebbles in five groups, each comprising five, two, three, two, and three rocks. The garden contains 15 rocks arranged on the surface of white pebbles in such a manner that visitors can see only 14 of them at once, no matter what angle the garden is viewed from. It is said that only when you attain spiritual enlightenment as a result of deep Zen meditation, can you see the last invisible stone.

www.yamasa.org/japan/english/destinations/kyoto/ryoanji.html

Chapter 6

The Ryoan-ji Rock Garden, Kyoto

The Zen rock garden (kare sansui) is one of the most well known iconic images of the spiritual side of Japan (as contrasted with the modern popular culture side of Japan reflected in the ubiquitous neon lights and manga). The garden is, like many Japanese gardens, made up of rocks, pebbles, and raked sand. The Ryoan-ji rock garden in Kyoto is probably the most famous rock garden in Japan and is generally considered a masterpiece of Japanese culture. In his book, *The Enduring Art of Japan,* Langdon Warner discusses the spiritual aspects of these gardens (1952:96–97):

> The fundamental thing about Japanese gardens, and what sets them apart from any other gardens of the civilized world, is usually lost sight of by Westerners. It is the fact that the art was definitely used in China and Japan to express the highest truths of religion and philosophy precisely as other civilizations have made use of the arts of literature and painting, of ritual dance and music.

He adds that westerners seem to vaguely recognize this matter, though they are primarily attracted by the austerity and pristine beauty of the gardens.

Characteristics of Japanese Rock Gardens

Let me say something about the characteristics of rock gardens. According to Gouverneur Mosher, author of *Kyoto: A Contemplative Guide,* rock gardens have three characteristics:

- first, they are small;
- second, they are monochromatic, and
- third, they are separated from other areas, with strong and well delineated boundaries.

These gardens are, then, excellent examples of Japanese minimalism, but this minimalism has interesting psychological aspects to it. That is because the very simplicity of these gardens creates all kinds of feelings in people who view them. As Mosher writes (1980:116–117):

The origins of rock gardens seem to be clear: they appeared at a time when black-and-white painting, having been imported to Japan from China, was creating great interest, as was simultaneously the art of "tray landscape" design. The application of these influences to garden design produced gardens in monochrome and in miniature. Because it was meant to be symbolic, a rock garden had to be small, lest its symbolism approach reality too closely and break down. Because it was small, this garden had to be clearly outlined. It was usually placed next to a building, as it tended to get lost in natural surroundings.

Typically, the gardens are limited in size, color, and environment. Usually a garden consists of little more that plain rocks set into a bed of white gravel. The main virtue of these gardens is permanence, for such gardens are not easily destroyed. However beyond that, the limitations of the form would seem to be too great to allow any range or depth of expression. In fact, what happens is just the reverse. The symbolism in these gardens is nearly unlimited, and that is because of their very simplicity and plainness—they open themselves up to an endless variety of interpretations.

Morris sees these gardens as similar in nature to modern painting, such as abstract expressionist paintings that might also be limited to black and white or just a few colors. Less "data" in abstract expressionist works creates more profound feelings and many different, and in some cases conflicting, interpretations.

Islands of serenity set off from the chaos of modern Japanese society, these rock gardens reflect the Japanese sensibility of being an island nation separated from other countries, whose values and practices are believed to pose dangers to a highly distinctive Japanese culture and character. The gardens are "islands" in Japan just as Japan is an island in the greater world, and the gardens are quintessentially Japanese in nature. They have a curious visual quality, for though they are small and confined, their spatiality conveys a sense of grandeur. The rocks represent islands and the raked sand represents waves. So there is an illusion of spatiality in these gardens because the scale of the rocks and sand is so perfect. The gardens are microcosms representing in a compressed scale a macrocosm, something very large—islands jutting out of huge seas. From a semiotic perspective, the Ryoan-ji rock garden and all rock gardens are superb examples of synecdoche: a part that represents the whole.

In their book, *A Guide to the Gardens of Kyoto,* Mark Treib and Ron Herman discuss the way these rock gardens offer respite to foreign travelers and enable them to "time travel" and gain a sense of what Japan was like in earlier days (1980:viii):

> The confusion or distancing from understanding caused by the modern Japanese metropolis is less acute in historic architecture and gardens, which are certainly more sympathetic in feeling. Quiet and repose are still found there in contrast to the density, bustle and noise of city life. In the historical gardens of Kyoto one slips back centuries to an ordered world of calm and balance.

We must be careful not to generalize too much and assume that these gardens and other refined or "elite" aspects of Japanese culture are widely popular there. That is because many modern Japanese people are more involved with their manga, movies, video games, cell phones and other aspects of Japanese popular culture than they are with elite "old" Japanese culture. Essentially, this Japanese historic or traditional culture exists for some Japanese and, in large measure, for tourists. It is the distinctive and refined esthetic sensibility of Japanese culture, as reflected in Japanese gardens, temples, forts, and what we might call Japanese traditional culture, that is so attractive to foreign tourists and one of the main reasons they visit Japan.

It is often the case that people who live in important tourist destinations, with world-famous monuments or other interesting sites, pay little attention to these sites. People generally are immersed in their everyday lives and tend to neglect world-famous sites where they live—perhaps because they think that someday they will visit them. It also may be that they've visited these sites when they were schoolchildren and thus they don't feel the need to visit them again. As an example of the way people put off visiting important tourist sites where they live, I've lived in the San Francisco bay area since 1970, and I have never been to Alcatraz, the number one tourist attraction in San Francisco, though I keep telling myself that one day I'll go there.

How Japanese Rock Gardens Work

The Yamasa Institute website, which provided the quotation that I used to begin this chapter, offers an explanation of how the Zen garden works. In its webpage we read the following about the garden:

> To understand its effect, and its purity, you have to go there. The design generates tension, drawing the viewer to contemplate the mystery of

Zen. It can't be photographed in entirety, the dimensions could drive any photographer to distraction, but that's the beauty of it. All you can do is just put the camera away, sit down and contemplate it. Especially when you realize that no matter where you sit, you will only see 14 of the rocks at any one time. The longer you sit, the more the garden fascinates. The branches of the trees beyond the earthen wall with its peculiar but natural designs are "borrowed scenery"—they bend and straighten, they cast fantastic shadows with the moss that fills the pocks and spaces in the rocks. The raked lines are circles around the rock groups and yet straight elsewhere—and you will love how the lines stop without a single misplaced pebble when they touch the circular patterns, and then resume unchanged beyond them as if the rocks are islands. It changes with the seasons—cherry trees beyond the wall blooming in spring, snow clinging to the moss in the winter. It is never the same twice. And although the rocks do not move, there is something about those spaces between the rocks. (www.yamasa.org/japan/english/destinations/kyoto/ryoanji.html)

The garden has the same qualities of abstract expressionist paintings, discussed above, that enable us to have emotional responses to what we see. When I visited the garden I was surprised by the effect it was having on the tourists who were contemplating it. There were people from many different countries and they regarded the garden with a kind of reverence one feels in the presence of the sacred. Was that due to the impact of the garden itself or some combination of what they had read about the garden—that is, the markers—and the actual impact of the garden? That question can be asked about all the icons in this book.

Japan, due to its island status and because it was isolated for so many years, developed a distinctive culture. This culture remains here and there in Japan—in Zen rock gardens, ancient forts, and other old buildings, and in certain areas of cities, but like the wonderful rock gardens of Japan, this traditional Japanese culture is isolated from contemporary everyday Japanese life. The Tokyo subway system, that serves millions of people every day, might be seen as the exemplary opposite of the rock gardens—two remarkably different aspects of the same distinctive culture.

The Tower is friendly. The Tower is also present to the entire world. First of all as a universal symbol of Paris, it is everywhere on the globe where Paris is to be stated as an image; from the Midwest to Australia, there is no journey to France which isn't made, somehow, in the Tower's name, no schoolbook, poster, or film about France which fails to propose it as the major sign of a people and of a place: it belongs to the universal language of travel.

Further: beyond its strictly Parisian statement, it touches the most general human image-repertoire: its simple, primary shape confers upon it the vocation of an infinite cipher: in turn and according to the appeals of our imagination, the symbol of Paris, of modernity, of communication, of science or of the nineteenth century, rocket, stem, derrick, phallus, lightning rod or insect, confronting the great itineraries of our dreams, it is the inevitable sign; just as there is no Parisian glance which is not compelled to encounter it, there is no fantasy which fails, sooner or later, to acknowledge its form and to be nourished by it; pick up a pencil and let your hand, in other words your thoughts, wander, and it is often the Tower which will appear, reduced to that simple line whose sole mythic function is to join, as the poet says, base and summit, or again, earth and heaven.

This pure—virtually empty—sign is ineluctable, because it means everything. In order to negate the Eiffel Tower (though the temptation to do so is rare, for this symbol offends nothing in us), you must, like Maupassant, get up on it and, so to speak, identify yourself with it.

Roland Barthes, *The Eiffel Tower and Other Mythologies.*

Chapter 7

The Eiffel Tower, Paris

For Roland Barthes, whose essay on the Eiffel Tower begins this chapter, the Eiffel Tower is a "pure" signifier that attracts attempts to understand its meaning and symbolic significance "the way a lightning rod attracts thunderbolts." His use of metaphor is particularly telling, since the interpretations by scholars of the meanings of the Eiffel Tower are so numerous that writing that it is like a lightning rod helps us understand one aspect of the role this structure plays in French life. It is a lightning rod

for analyses and interpretations of the significance of the Eiffel Tower by scholars with many different points of view about its symbolic significance and cultural meaning.

The Mythic Significance of the Eiffel Tower

In his essay, Barthes discusses the mythic significance of the Tower and relates it to the Biblical myth of the Tower of Babel, but suggests that it is a variation of the myth based on mankind's desire to communicate with God, not storm the heavens the way the original Tower of Babel story in the Bible described its function. The world "Babel" is similar to the Hebrew word for "jumble." God confounded mankind by making people speak many languages and making it difficult for them to understand one another and mount an assault on the heavens.

We can make a rough analogy between the scattering of languages and the seemingly infinite variety of interpretations of the social and cultural significance of the Eiffel Tower. When the Eiffel Tower was built, we must remember, it was the tallest building in the world and was seen as an architectural triumph—though, for many French people at the time, it was considered to be an ugly building. It was built in 1889 for the Universal Exposition in Paris and was meant to be a memorial for the 100th anniversary of the French Revolution and a signifier of human progress and solidarity.

A Psychoanalytic Perspective on the Eiffel Tower

From a psychoanalytic perspective, it is, like all towers, connected to unconscious desires in men to construct buildings that signify their phallic power. Before Freud, people did not recognize that the towers they created were connected to their sexual drives. Now, in an age when psychoanalytic theory has become widespread, seeing towers, sky scrapers, and other very tall structures as having a phallic significance does not seem far-fetched—except, of course, to those hostile to the notion of an unconscious and psychoanalytic theory. The popular notion that the French are "sexy" may be connected to unconscious derivatives of the tower's phallic and "penetrating" nature. If there is a womb symbol in Paris, it might be the catacombs or some other "feminine" incorporating structure.

In an article by Don Wellman on "The Birth of Modernism," we discover the Eiffel Tower is intimately connected with human sexuality. He writes:

7. *The Eiffel Tower, Paris*

The Tower is a human silhouette; with no head, if not a fine needle, and without arms... it is nevertheless a long torso placed on two legs spread apart.... But here again the camera eye discovers a new truth of the Tower, that of an object that has a sex. In the great unleashing of symbols, the phallus is no doubt its simplest figuration; but through the perspective of the photograph, it is the whole interior of the Tower, projected against the sky, that appears streaked by the pure forms of sex. (faculty.dwc.edu/wellman/Birth__Modernism.html)

He points out that Barthes had a more complicated analysis of the Eiffel Tower and writes "Barthes discovers a mandala-like, female sexual essence in the pattern of girders as seen from below against the sky. The Tower for him is both sexes intertwined or all sex, rather than reductively only the phallus."

The sexual nature of the Eiffel tower, and all towers, is, from a psychoanalytic perspective, felt at the unconscious level. At the conscious level, the Eiffel tower is a building, but at the unconscious level, its sexual significance becomes meaningful. And that is because, as Freud suggested, the similarity between a penis and a tall building resonates in our psyches.

The Eiffel Tower and the Myth Model

Over the years I've developed what I describe as a "Myth Model" that looks at the way specific myths are reflected in and inform psychoanalytic theory, historical events, elite culture, popular culture, and everyday life. Let me use this "Myth Model" to deal with the myth of the Tower of Babel and the Eiffel Tower.

MYTH	TOWER OF BABEL
Psychoanalytic Theory	Phallic Symbols
Historical Events	Building Skyscrapers
Elite Culture	Barthes essay. Walter Benjamin, etc.
Popular Culture	Films: *A View to Kill, Lavender Hill Mob, Zazie dans Le Metro,* etc.
	Half size replica of Eiffel tower in Las Vegas
Everyday Life	Visit the Eiffel Tower

As might be expected, the Eiffel Tower is seen in every film that takes place in Paris and has also been found in various video games and novels. Barthes suggests the phallic nature of the Eiffel Tower in his classic essay. Anyone who has read Freud can understand how towers, along with many other objects or buildings that represent the penis in form and function, can be understood as being phallic symbols.

Walter Benjamin has some citations in his *The Arcades Project* about the Eiffel Tower and the development of iron buildings. One by Dubech and d'Espezel in their book *Histoire de Paris* captures the feeling of many people when the tower was first constructed:

> Greeted at first by a storm of protest, it has remained quite ugly though it proved useful for research on wireless telegraphy...It has been said that this world exhibition marked the triumph of iron construction. It would be truer to say that it marked its bankruptcy. (1999:161)

Benjamin's citations on the Eiffel Tower show that it was considered an ugly monstrosity when it was constructed. Now, of course, it is considered a beautiful building that signifies Paris and France.

The Complexity of Analyzing Cultural Icons

What these different interpretations of the Eiffel Tower demonstrate is that cultural icons are very complicated phenomena. In her analysis of cultural icons, "The Eiffel Tower: Cultural Icon, Cultural Interface" (in Keyan G. Tomaselli and David Scott, editors, *Cultural Icons*), Stephanie A. Glaser deals with the complexities of writing about cultural icons such as the Eiffel Tower (2009:61):

> Because symbolic and nationalistic meanings were imposed upon it even before its completion, its iconic status has always been related to, as well as confused with, its function as a national symbol. Most importantly, the tower appeared at a decisive historical moment. Engendered by the emerging industrial society, its meanings were constructed by that society and its spin-offs: consumerism, public transport, mechanical reproduction, print culture.

From its beginning, then, the Eiffel Tower played an important role in France as a national symbol and as an icon connected to the development of consumer culture (think of all the key chains and other trinkets based on the Eiffel Tower) and of the tourism industry. In 2010, some 6.7

million people visited the Eiffel Tower, making it one of the most important tourism destinations in Paris. France receives more international tourists than any other country. There were more than 76 million visitors to France in 2010, and 42 million of those tourists spent time in Paris and its suburbs. The Eiffel Tower is also, of course, a universal symbol of France, or what Barthes would call "Frenchness," though it is really more directly an icon of Paris and all that is attached to Paris in the popular imagination. Because we see the Eiffel Tower in so many films, television shows, or televised news reports about Paris, metonymically we associate the tower with Paris and France. There are 41,800,000 citations in Google for the Eiffel Tower, so we can see it is a building with enormous cultural relevance and resonance.

Theorizing Tourism: Analyzing Iconic Destinations by Arthur Asa Berger, 80–85.

Passing through Las Vegas is Route 91, the archetype of the commercial strip, the phenomenon at its purest and most intense. We believe careful documentation and analysis of its physical form is as important to architects and urbanists today as were the studies of medieval Europe and ancient Rome to earlier generations.... Signs in Las Vegas use mixed media—words, pictures and sculpture—to persuade and inform. A sign is contradictorily for day and night. The same sign works as polychromic sculpture in the sun and as black silhouette against the sun; at night it is a source of light. It revolves by day and becomes a play of lights at night. It contains scales for close up and distance.... Day is negated inside the casinos and night negated on the Strip. The signs are, contradictorily, for day and night.

Robert Venturi, Steven Izenour, and Denise Scott Brown, *Learning from Las Vegas: Revised Edition: On Forgotten Symbolism of Architectural Form*

As Venturi and associates have pointed out, competition in thematic displays always leads to larger and more spectacular signs. This is certainly the case in recent years as casinos have shifted to staged productions, simulations, and other spectacular forms such as theme parks and immense statues like the sphinx in front of the Luxor and the lion entrance to the MGM Grand. Such intense competition over themes has also produced a new Las Vegas experience centered, not on the exterior play of fantasy differences among casinos, but within the constructed space itself. By catering to the growing market of family visitors, several casinos have built immense theme parks that offer Disney-style rides and attractions.

Mark Gottdiener, *The Theming of America: Visions, Dreams and Commercial Spaces*

Chapter 8

The Las Vegas Strip, Nevada

There is, we have been told in an influential book, a lot to learn from Las Vegas. Robert Venturi, Steven Izenour, and Denise Scott Brown describe the strip as follows in their book *Learning from Las Vegas* (1977:20):

> The image of the commercial strip is chaos. The order in this landscape is not obvious…the continuous highway itself and its systems for turning are absolutely consistent…the median strip accommodates the U-turns necessary to a vehicular promenade for casino crawling as well as left turns onto the local street pattern that the Strip intercepts.

Las Vegas may have a lot to teach architects and urbanists, but its claim to fame is that it is a city devoted to gambling (now called "gaming" to give itself a bit of respectability), a city that is full of hotels that are the epitome of excess (many of the earlier ones were examples of gangster chic), and a city

that prides itself on keeping its dirty secrets. "What happens in Las Vegas stays in Las Vegas," we are told in advertisements for the city.

In the popular imagination, Las Vegas is a classic signifier of sin, lust, and abandon, since it is a location where gambling and illicit sex are of central importance. It appeals to and loosens id elements in our psyches—a matter I will discuss shortly—and has a history that involves gangsters owning and designing casinos and hotels and playing an important role in the city. Las Vegas is a city where risk dominates and where the darker elements in human beings are encouraged. And it promises that nobody will find out what you do in Las Vegas, which encourages kinds of behavior (gambling, illicit sex) that are self-destructive.

The travel writer Jan Morris picked up on an aspect of Las Vegas connected to its penchant for keeping secrets. She writes about Las Vegas as "Fun City" in *Journeys* (1984:32) and sees a rather dark and sinister side to the city:

> Fun City is no fun really, after a day or two, and when the Vegas operators speak of fun, they are using double-speak. The days when the Mafia ran Vegas were Fun Days—the Good Old Days of criminals like Bugsie Malone [*sic*] and Moe Sedway—the "legendary characters" of Vegas, the "old guys." In the garden of the Flamingo Hotel, now a Hilton, an inscription facetiously suggests that its roses may flourish so brightly because Bugsie [*sic*] buried missing victims there; but there is nothing funny really to the hidden meanings of Las Vegas, its brutal subsoil and its often sinister compost.
>
> Sinister? The adept manipulations of brilliant businessmen? The enterprising vulgarities of Circus Circus? The tinsel of the wedding chapels? Swinging Suz's, which features Black, English and other Exotic Escorts? Ah, but there is to the very presence of Las Vegas, I came to feel by the end of my stay, a suggestion of true evil. This is more than a discreet city, where photography is not encouraged and anonymity is respected: it is a profoundly secret one.

For Morris, beneath the glitter of Las Vegas there was a rather ugly core, and her feelings about Las Vegas captured the feelings of many people who see it not as a "fun" city but as a tragic and sad one. For Morris, the symbols of Las Vegas are the gray concrete walls that surround people's homes and the bizarre, agoraphobic Howard Hughes, who lived on the ninth floor of his hotel, the Desert Inn, and owned, at one time, many hotels in Las Vegas.

Tom Wolfe picks up on an important aspect of the Las Vegas strip—namely that the city is dominated by signs. As he writes in his essay "Las Vegas (What?)" in *The Kandy-Kolored Tangerine-Flake Streamline Baby* (1966:7):

> Las Vegas is the only town in the world whose skyline is made up neither of buildings, like New York, nor of trees, like Wilbraham, Massachusetts, but signs. One can look at Las Vegas from a mile away on Route 91 and see no buildings, no trees, only signs. But such signs! They tower. They revolve, they oscillate, the soar in shapes before which the existing vocabulary of art history is helpless. I can only attempt to supply names—Boomerang Modern, Palette Curvilinear, Flash Gordon Ming-Alert Spiral, McDonald's Hamburger Parabola, Mint Casino Elliptical, Miami Beach Kidney.

Wolfe's list of types of signs connects them to American popular culture and to phenomena such as the ubiquitous McDonald's hamburger restaurants. The signs, and many of the hotels, reflect the aesthetic of the gangsters who owned many hotels and were responsible for the signs that advertised them. A sixteen-story sign that soars above a two story building transcends its origin and becomes, though it may be vulgar, an aesthetic statement of its own.

Las Vegas, epitomized by its famous strip and hotels/casinos, can be seen as a kind of sanctuary area for gambling, promiscuous sex, entertainment (formerly Liberace, now think Celine Dion) and, it would seem, anything else one might think of or desire. Excess is the style on the Las Vegas strip. It also now has some of the best and most expensive restaurants in the United States.

Psychoanalytic Theory and Las Vegas

It is possible to think of gambling in terms of Sigmund Freud's analysis of the human psyche. His first such analysis focused upon the different layers in the human mind. We can see this in the form of an iceberg floating in the sea.

Above the water we see the tip of the iceberg, which represents consciousness—what we are aware of in our minds. Just below the water is a blurry area of

CONSCIOUS

SUBCONSCIOUS

UNCONSCIOUS

around six feet that represents the subconscious—material in our minds that we can bring to consciousness under the right circumstances.

But below that area, and representing around 85 percent of the iceberg, we find a dark area, the unconscious. We cannot access it without help from psychologists and psychoanalysts, but the unconscious has a profound effect on our behavior. It is material buried in the unconscious of gamblers that helps explain their self-destructive behavior.

Freud later developed a second theory of the psyche that helps us understand cities like Las Vegas. He suggested that there is a battle in the human psyche between three forces: the Id, the Ego, and the Superego. These forces contend at the unconscious level.

The Id represents desire, lust, "I want it all now."

The Ego focuses upon reality and tries to mediate between the Id and the Superego.

The Superego represents guilt and conscience.

The Id gives us energy, but if not controlled, we become victims of our random desires. The Superego helps guide us, but if it is too strong and dominates our Ids too much, we cannot act and have no energy. And the Ego works to prevent the Id or Superego from becoming dominant and keeps us on an even keel.

We can take Freud's typology and use its components to classify various cities:

ID	EGO	SUPEREGO
Drives	Rationality	Guilt
Sex, Gambling	Logic	Religion
Las Vegas	Boston	Vatican City

I put Boston as an Ego city because it has so many colleges and universities. Education is essentially an ego function. The Vatican City is the home of the Roman Catholic Church, which, like most religions, is the source of our superego-induced sense of guilt. And it is the fact that the Las Vegas Strip is seen as a place where we can freely indulge the Id forces in our psyches that is an important part of its attraction.

LAS VEGAS STATISTICS FOR 2009:

36,351,469 visitors

148,000 rooms

Occupancy rate: 81.5%

Average daily room rate: $92.93

Las Vegas has the distinction of being the second most popular tourist attraction in the United States—in terms of the number of people who visit attractions. Its hotel occupancy rate is very high: 81.5% compared to Orlando (home of Disney World) at 60.7% and Chicago at 56.6%. Las Vegas is exceeded only, in popularity for tourists—both foreign and domestic—by Times Square. But New York City has 8 million inhabitants and around 45 million visitors in a given year, and Las Vegas has 550,000 inhabitants—in Nevada, a state with a total population of 2.5 million. The fact that Las Vegas attracts more than 36 million visitors a year is a testimonial to the Strip's awesome drawing power, to our desire to escape the constraints of our superegos and free our ids to enjoy various pleasures—and to the comforting fact that what happens in Las Vegas supposedly stays in Las Vegas.

Las Vegas as a Postmodern Pastiche of Other Cultures

And for those who want a bit of sophistication and "class," it has a hotel complex, Paris-Las Vegas, which features a half-sized version—about 500 feet or forty stories high—of the Eiffel Tower. In a sense, Las Vegas allows visitors there to be "world tourists," in that they can visit many important tourists sites and buildings, in scaled down imitations, in one place. They can see the Sphinx, Times Square, and the Eiffel Tower in one afternoon. These simulations remind us that authenticity doesn't mean much for postmodern tourists, who want to be amused and entertained and don't care whether the sites they visit are authentic or simulations. Las Vegas becomes, then, a pastiche-like collection of world-class tourist sites all jumbled together in various themed hotels. The pastiche, postmodern thinkers remind us, is the basic postmodern art form. By using themed hotels (Egypt, Paris, and so forth) the companies that built these hotels were able to differentiate themselves from other hotels on the strip and develop a distinctive identity. These themed hotels also benefitted from the auras of the places they imitated and from what we might describe as the "halo" effect provided by the imitated tourist destinations.

Why settle for the real thing and all the expense involved in traveling to Paris or Egypt, we may ask as postmodernist tourists, when you can have the imitation and it doesn't cost very much to see—unless, that is, you develop a fondness for slot machines!

Theorizing Tourism: Analyzing Iconic Destinations by Arthur Asa Berger, 86–91.

Though it's known to everyone as St. Basil's, this legendary building is officially called "The Cathedral of the Intercession of the Virgin by the Moat". The popular alternative refers to Basil the Blessed, a Muscovite 'holy fool' who was buried on the site (in the Trinity Cathedral that once stood here) a few years before the present building was erected. The Cathedral was ordered by Ivan the Terrible to mark the 1552 capture of Kazan from Mongol forces. It was completed in 1560. That's pretty much all the genuine history that's known about this celebrated landmark. There [are], however, scores of legends. Nothing is known about the builders, Barma and Postnik Yakovlev, except their names and the dubious legend that Ivan had them blinded so that they could not create anything to compare. Historians unanimously state that this is nothing but urban folklore. Architectural specialists are to this day unable to agree about the governing idea behind the structure. Either the creators were paying homage to the churches of Jerusalem, or, by building eight churches around a central ninth, they were representing the medieval symbol of the eight-pointed star. The original concept of the Cathedral of the Intercession has been hidden from us beneath layers of stylistic additions and new churches added to the main building. In fact, when built, the Cathedral was all white to match the white-stone Kremlin, and the onion domes were gold rather than multi-colored and patterned as they are today. In the 17th century a hip-roofed bell tower was added, the gallery and staircases were covered with vaulted roofing, and the helmeted domes were replaced with decorated ones. In 1860 during rebuilding, the Cathedral was painted with a more complex and integrated design, and has remained unchanged since. The Cathedral is now a museum. One service a year is held in the Cathedral, on the Day of Intercession in October.

www.moscow.info/red-square/st-basils-cathedral.aspx

Chapter 9

St. Basil's Cathedral in Red Square, Moscow

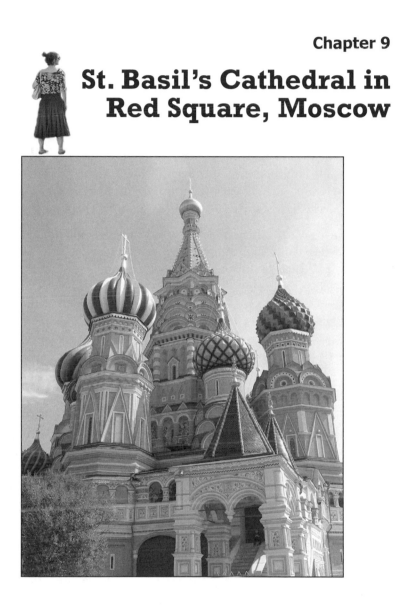

In *The Dialogic Imagination: Four Essays by M.M. Bakhtin,* edited by Michael Holquist, we find discussions of the role of the fool, along with the roles of the rogue and the clown, all of whom played roles in the development of the European novel. Everything these characters do must be interpreted metaphorically because their actions function as critiques of the societies in which they find themselves. As Bakhtin explains (1981:161):

> Opposed to convention and functioning as a force for exposing it, we have the level-headed, cheery and clever wit of the rogue…the parodied taunts of the clown and the simpleminded incomprehension of the fool. Opposed to ponderous and gloomy deception we have the rogue's cheerful deceit, opposed to greedy falsehood and hypocrisy we have the fool's unselfish simplicity and his healthy failure to understand; opposed to everything that is conventional and false, we have the clown—a sympathetic form for the (parodied) exposure of others.

We may say, then, that St. Basil's Cathedral provides an architecturally symbolic balance to the heaviness of Red Square and the Communist political order that dominated Russia for so many years. The cathedral is a reminder of the comic element in Russian life that has existed over the centuries, as a counterweight to the burdens of the czar, the church, and the Communist government. And it's not only Russian Communism, but the Russian "character" that this critiques. The humor of self parody, attacking the heaviness of Russian life and culture.

St. Basil's and Whimsy

One thing that is curious about the cathedral is that there is an element of whimsy about it—having all those onion domes and painting them all those colors contrasts with the heaviness of Red Square, with its huge Kremlin and GUM shopping mall.. The buildings in Red Square are mostly made of red brick. They are ornate and elegant, but they lack the pizzazz of the cathedral. The coloration of the cathedral calls to mind the many beautiful ikons found in Russian Orthodox cathedrals. In St. Basil's, like other Orthodox cathedrals, most of the wall space is covered with colorful ikons (including one of Ivan the Terrible), and this feeling for color found in the ikons may have played a role in the coloration of the onion domes of the building.

An article in *The Guardian* compares it to England's *Fawlty Towers*, the TV show. "That Was Fawlty Towers" mentions the cathedral's "symbolic power" as being important:

> Was it St Basil's symbolic power that led to its persecution, or simply its comedy aesthetics? Even without the garish candy colour scheme (it was originally white), it's an odd-looking pile-up of onion domes, polygonal

towers, *blank* arches and sharp spires and extremes of architectural vocabulary. Little is known about its architect, Postnik Yakovlev. Perhaps he was a children's entertainer whom Ivan the Terrible enlisted in a rare moment of levity. Ivan's predecessor, Ivan III, had imported an Italian Renaissance architect, Aristotele Fioravanti, to design his Cathedral of the Dormition at the Kremlin (not that it really shows), but historians have scrabbled around to find a precedent for St Basil's. (www.guardian.co.uk/ artanddesign/2011/jul/12/st-basil-s-cathedral-russia-google-doodle)

This symbolic power, as a kind of antidote to Russian melancholy, might explain why the cathedral is such a tourist attraction.

The Power of Aesthetics

What catches your attention first when you see St. Basil's Cathedral is how striking it is. It is the multi-colored and patterned onion domes that catch your attention. If they were white, the way they were originally colored, or even covered with gold, the building would not be as remarkable as it is. St. Basil's Cathedral is also an old building—built between 1555 and 1561. It is located in the geometric center of Moscow, which radiates in all directions from the cathedral. It is, we might say, at the heart of Moscow, which means it is at the heart of Russia. Since most tourists who visit Russia have seen images of the cathedral in books, magazines, and television news reports, when they are there and actually see it, the impression is very powerful.

Tourists derive a great deal of pleasure from visiting iconic buildings and places, from being at them and being able to photograph them. That feeling, I suggest, is one of the reasons that people travel. When you visit Red Square you see tourists snapping pictures one after another of the cathedral, as if they were afraid it was going to vanish. As I explained in Chapter 2, one of the things tourists do is take photographs of the places they visit. I quoted Stanley Milgram, a social psychologist, who suggested that photography has changed the meaning of travel and that many tourists visit sites because of their importance as "photo opportunities." He suggested that there was a trade-off between enjoying a particular scene and photographing it, and that the process of taking photographs may interfere with the enjoyment of the place being visited. Places, then, become secondary to their photographic potentialities, and it is the search for good photo opportunities that motivates many tourists, though they may not recognize as much. Many tourists include their partners or themselves in their photos to show that they actually visited a given site and to provide a record of sorts to help them remember the experiences they had when there.

The fact that the cathedral has survived for more than 450 years is considered by many people to be miraculous. There are stories that Stalin protected it from his generals, who wanted to tear it down so Russian troops on parade could more easily exit from Red Square, and that Stalin wanted to destroy it but was dissuaded from doing so by a famous Russian architect Baranovsky, who stood on the cathedral's steps and threatened to cut his throat if the church was demolished. The cathedral was spared, but Baranovsky spent five years in prison for his actions.

St. Basil's as a Metonym

The survival of St. Basil's may be taken as a symbol for the survival of Russia, which, over the centuries, was the object of massive invasions by many nations, such as Sweden and Poland in earlier times and other countries in more recent times. The most serious threats to Russia's existence as a sovereign nation were by Napoleon in the nineteenth century and Hitler in the twentieth century, during the Second World War.

St. Basil's, we may say, is a "holy fool of buildings" and functions as a signifier and a metonym of Russia and all things Russian. It suggests a dimension of Russian culture and character of which many people are unaware. There is no building anywhere else in the world that is like it (except a replica, one third the size, in a small Russian city). It also leads us to consider the role of the Orthodox Church in Russia. In his book *The Russians,* Hedrick Smith discusses the complicated relationship that exists between the Russian Orthodox Church and the government. He writes (1976:436):

> The relation between the Church and the Party is a curious one. As an institution vigorously repressed in the Twenties and Thirties, allowed to revive by Stalin during World War II to rally Russian patriotism, and later roughly suppressed by Khrushchev, the Orthodox Church has accepted uneasy accommodation with the Brezhnev leadership. Throughout Russian history, the Orthodox establishment has reinforced secular power by preaching submission to the state among its faithful.

Long suppressed, by Communist leaders, the Russian Orthodox Church now is flourishing having reached an accommodation with contemporary Russian politicians like Vladimir Putin, who find an alliance with the church to be useful.

9. St. Basil's Cathedral in Red Square, Moscow

Saint Basil's cathedral, semiotically speaking, is a powerful signifier of the comedic aspects of Russian national character and functions as a counterpoint to the heaviness of the other buildings in Red Square. In Red Square we have the two opposing poles of Russian character combined in one site. Tourists who go to Russia visit many other beautiful Russian Orthodox cathedrals, but none is as remarkable as Saint Basil's and none has the power that Saint Basil's has to stand as a signifier of "Russian-ness," of Russian character and culture.

Theorizing Tourism: Analyzing Iconic Destinations by Arthur Asa Berger, 92–97.

A small-ship expedition to Antarctica might be the single greatest adventure travel opportunity of your life. We're proud to say that in 1966, Lindblad became the first to offer expedition travel to Antarctica. That's over 40 years of experience in the most wild place on earth. So we understand fully the responsibility as well as the potential for life changing experiences that this vast landscape carries. No mere drive-by, our Antarctica expedition cruises go deeper. You'll have the opportunity to travel with National Geographic experts and the most experienced Ice Team on earth. With their leadership, step foot on land overflowing with life. Zodiac past soaring icebergs. Kayak in protected waters, padding around icebergs as penguins swim by. And encounter Antarctica from the safety and comfort of our new expedition ship, National Geographic Explorer.

Lindblad website: expeditions.com/Destination44.a

No place on earth compares to this vast white wilderness distilled to an elemental haiku: snow, ice, water, rock. Antarctica is simply stunning. The enormity of its ice shelves and mountain ranges invariably heightens feelings of humanity's insignificance and nature's grandeur. Antarctica's peculiar beauty may haunt you for the rest of your days. Even the trip over, crossing the Southern Ocean, is an experience—with no landmass, low-pressure systems circle clockwise unimpeded, eventually reaching incredible speeds. The Falkland Islands in the South Atlantic are often included in a trip to Antarctica. Because the continent has never had a native population—even today, scientists and other staff members at research stations are only temporary residents—Antarctic wildlife is still unafraid of people. Well-behaved visitors usually elicit no more than disinterested yawns from seals and penguins focused on rearing their young and evading predators. The human reaction is exactly opposite: almost all visitors to Antarctica find that their experiences here exceed their expectations. Everyone—scientist, support worker, government official and tourist alike—who comes to this, the most isolated continent, must 'earn' Antarctica, either by making an often-difficult voyage or a costly flight. Ice and weather, not clocks or calendars, determine the itinerary and the timetable of all travel here.

www.lonelyplanet.com/antarctica

Chapter 10

Antarctic

Why is seeing Antarctica and landing on the Antarctic continent so important to people? The passion shown by many of the passengers on a cruise I took to Antarctica made me wonder whether there might be an unrecognized sacred or hidden religious dimension to the voyage. Could it be that many of the passengers, without fully recognizing what they were doing, were on some kind of a religious pilgrimage and that Antarctica's incredible natural beauty was similar, in nature, to the sacred destinations of many religious pilgrims?

The Sacred and the Profane

In his book *The Sacred and The Profane: The Nature of Religion,* Eliade (1961) argues that for religious people, time and space are seen differently from the way they are seen by non-religious people. Thus, for religious men and women, there are some spaces that can be described as sacred—think of churches, synagogues, temples, and certain areas in countries where religious ceremonies are held. These places are seen as quite different from profane, everyday places. Eliade (1961:116) writes:

> For religious man, nature is never only 'natural'; it is always fraught with religious value. This is easy to understand, for the cosmos is a divine creation; coming from the hands of the gods, the world is impregnated with sacredness. It is not simply a sacrality *communicated* by the gods, as is the case, for example, with a place or an object consecrated by the divine presence. The gods did more; *They manifested the different modalities of the sacred in the very structure of the world and of cosmic phenomena.*

So, sailing to Antarctica can be interpreted, if we keep Eliade's ideas in mind, as involving a visit to sacred space and an attempt to establish a more harmonious relationship with nature and with God. There may also be an element, not recognized by the passengers, of a search for paradise and for some kind of a Shangri-La in visiting Antarctica, except that the Shangri-La the visitors to Antarctica are seeking exists not in the Himalayas, but in their imaginations, hidden away somewhere in the vast wilderness of Antarctica's empty and mysterious interior. The ice and snow in Antarctica are pure and virginal, and except for the perimeter of the continent, seldom visited by human beings. Antarctica is, then, a kind of virgin land, unoccupied by humans (except for a few thousand scientists) and uncorrupted, for the most part, by civilization.

In addition to the regular or mainstream ocean cruise lines that sail in the waters of Antarctica, there are what we might describe as specialty lines—generally small "expedition" cruise ships with unusual itineraries—that take passengers to small ports in various countries and to polar regions such as Antarctica. The specialty lines that go to Antarctica have ships with reinforced hulls and other structural features to protect them from the ice, but they are not the only ones that sail in Antarctica's waters. A number of the mainstream lines, such as Princess and Holland America, sail through Antarctica waters, but they do not land passengers on the continent. According to an article in *The Encyclopedia of Ecotourism*, edited by David B. Weaver, the first scenic cruise to Antarctica with a 1,000 passenger ship was in 2000.

The International Association of Antarctica Tour Operators (IAATO) has strict rules about the number of people who can land in Antarctica at one time, which precludes large passenger liners from doing so. In addition, it can be difficult to land on Antarctica—you have to use small zodiac boats to get to the continent—so it would be impossible for large cruise liners with thousands of passengers to land them all on Antarctica even if they were allowed to do so. Most of the specialty expedition-style cruise vessels that land their passengers on Antarctica carry between 40 and 150 passengers.

A Mainstream Cruise to Antarctica on the *Star Princess*

People who take cruises tend to spend a great deal of time talking with other passengers at their dining tables. And one of their favorite topics is the cruises they have taken and the ones they are planning to take. Several people I met during our meals told me that this cruise in Antarctica waters was their "cruise of a lifetime." You have to do a good deal of sailing from Buenos Aires to reach Antarctica. We only landed at four ports during this cruise, but we spent a number of days cruising in Antarctica waters. The ports we visited were extremely interesting and provided the passengers with the chance to visit penguin colonies, see some beautiful scenery, and explore some remarkable sites.

On our cruise, the naturalist said that it was estimated that only 300,000 people had ever seen Antarctica and only 50,000 people had actually landed on Antarctica. There is reason to question these figures, since the IAATO claims that 46,000 people visited Antarctica and 30,000 people set foot on Antarctica in 2007–2008 alone. When we were in Antarctic waters, I wrote the following notes in my travel journal:

> The captain said today's the cleanest that he had ever seen Antarctica. He said that we are very lucky because some cruises are fogged in. He said we might expect a day like today just a few times a year. The mountains are remarkable … there are glaciers one after another … What is it about the scenery that is so mesmerizing? Perhaps it's the clarity of the mountains and the icebergs shimmering in the sun against a blue sky. The scenery today was incredible and adding to the experience was the realization that days like today are really rare.

I'm sure that everyone on board felt the same, because all the passengers were snapping photographs one after another, and exclaiming in excited voices how beautiful they found Antarctica's scenery.

While the idea of doing something adventurous or different may have motivated many of the passengers on the ship, I think it was their desire to see this pristine and spectacularly beautiful continent that was the major motivator. The scenery generated high spirits and blissful, almost ecstatic, reactions in most of the passengers. I wrote in my journal that after the cruise to Antarctica, I didn't feel that I wanted to take any more ocean cruises, because none of them could possibly match the Antarctic experience.

As I explained earlier, a relatively small number of people take cruises that allow them to go ashore on Antarctica. Given the nature of the Antarctic cruise experience, the marketers for the companies that sell cruises to the area use different strategies to position these cruises from those found for mainstream cruises that just sail in Antarctic waters. Most of the passengers on the ship I was on, the *Star Princess*, had taken other cruises and were looking for a somewhat different kind of cruise experience.

For some passengers, visiting Antarctica is part of a quest, and enabled them to check off one more continent in their attempt to visit all seven. During our cruise I met a number of people who sailed to Antarctica because they wanted to be able to say they had seen, visited, or spent time in all seven continents. One woman on the cruise told me that this cruise meant that she had been to (or seen) six continents and only had to visit Australia to complete her quest. What this shows is that tourists have many different motivations that explain their behavior. Tourists who visit Antarctica on mainstream cruise liners would be considered organized or individual mass tourists in Cohen's typology, while those who take cruises that enable them to land on the continent would be explorers, and in Plog's typology, allocentric tourists. There is an element of danger and a great deal of physical effort involved in visiting Antarctica, so you wouldn't expect psychocentric tourists to think of setting foot on it. Psychocentric tourists are not, by nature, adventure tourists. But adventure tourists to Antarctica go in groups; individuals cannot visit the continent on their own. Adventure tourism is not always an individual endeavor. Adventure tourists who climb Mount Everest go in groups and need large support staffs to make the climb possible. In my typology, this would refer to hierarchical elites, who have the financial resources to take a cruise that enables them to set foot on Antarctica. Landing on Antarctica, despite the hardships involved in visiting it, is a luxury that most people cannot afford.

Visiting Antarctica can also be seen as a kind of time travel, offering passengers an opportunity to experience what the world may have been like millions of years ago. For Antarctica is, whatever else it may be, a gigantic ice desert and wilderness. Most of the time Antarctica is a vast and empty continent, with an interior that very few people get to see. It is possible to fly to certain areas beyond the coast and land on Antarctica for short periods of time. A videotape I saw of a planeload of tourists to these regions on their return flight showed absolutely exhausted adventurers. They looked as if they were recovering from an ordeal, caused by the cold and wind during the very limited amount of time they spent on Antarctica.

The Myth Model and Antarctic Travel

Anthropologist and folklorist Raphael Patai suggests in *Myth and Modern Man* (1972) that there are unsuspected mythic motivations that shape much of our behavior. Eliade (1961) talks about camouflaged myths and makes the same argument. I have taken this notion that myths shape behavior and developed a model that enables us to see ways in which myths impact on various areas of our culture—I used it earlier to explain the significance of the Eiffel Tower for tourists. We can use this model to offer an explanation of why tourists go to Antarctica.

THE MYTH MODEL

Myth:	Dangerous voyage of Odysseus.
Historical Experience:	Amundsen, Shackelton, Byrd in Antarctica
Elite Culture:	Novel *Antarctic Navigation* by Elizabeth Arthur
Popular Culture:	Graphic Novel *Justice League Antarctica*
Everyday Life:	Tourists cruise by Antarctica and/or land on Antarctica

There may be a mythic impetus, of which we are unaware, behind our desire to see Antarctica or land on the continent.

The polar cruises website www.PolarCruises.com describes its "Expedition" Antarctic cruises as follows: "Expedition cruising began in 1966. This category of ship still adheres to the principles of conservation and preservation and world exploration for *the fortunate few*" [emphasis added]. We see, then, a note of elitism in this advertising copy. It is not simply "the few" who get to visit Antarctica, but the "fortunate few." The advertising copy for the Lindblad Antarctic cruise, with which this analysis began, suggests that a trip to Antarctica might be, and strongly implies that it will be, "the single greatest adventure travel opportunity of your life."

The Lindblad copy adds that the trip has "the potential for life changing experiences," so traveling to Antarctica with Lindblad, the first company to offer travel to Antarctica, promises great adventure and personal growth. It also offers security, since Lindblad has "the most experienced Ice Team on earth" to "the most wild place on earth." The language here is full of superlatives as Lindblad distances its expeditions—a term which suggests adventure and some kind of a lofty goal being pursued, such as exploration—from mere "drive-by" cruises such as those offered by Princess, Holland America, and other mainstream cruise lines, and from other cruise lines that offer expeditions to Antarctica.

The Fortunate Few and Antarctica's Good Fortune

Antarctica has fewer visitors than any other continent, in part because it is so remote and so cold and inhospitable most of the year. During the months when it is possible to visit the continent, more and more tourists are going there, though the number of those who cruise in its waters is small and the number of tourists who land on the continent is tiny compared to those who take cruises in the Caribbean or to Alaska. Antarctica's remoteness and the cost of visiting it may actually be a blessing because Antarctica has a very fragile environment, and large numbers of tourists would inevitably cause considerable damage. Not only is Antarctica a destination for "the fortunate few," it is fortunate, from a sustainable tourism perspective, that relatively few people go there.

Theorizing Tourism: Analyzing Iconic Destinations by Arthur Asa Berger, 98–105.

The charming city of Luang Prabang, once the capital of Laos and still considered to be its spiritual heart, breathes a rich meld of French Indochinese architecture, Theravada Buddhist temples and a magical atmosphere. Luang Prabang is strikingly situated on a peninsula formed by the confluence of two rivers, the Mekong and the Khan. Its palm-lined riverbanks, terracotta roofs, golden stupas and saffron-robed monks all come together to form a picture postcard increasingly difficult to find in Southeast Asia. Somnambulant and languid, its peaceful feel masks a history of conquest and recapture, and only hints at the intricate culture and traditional rituals that still take place here every day. Declared a UNESCO World Heritage site in 1995, the town was described by the global body as "an outstanding example of the fusion of traditional architecture and Lao urban structures with those built by the European colonial authorities in the 19th and 20th centuries. Its unique, remarkably well-preserved townscape illustrates a key stage in the blending of these two distinct cultural traditions."

www.travelfish.org/location/laos/northern_laos/luang_prabang/luang_prabang

Chapter 11

Luang Prabang, Laos

Luang Prabang, a UNESCO World Heritage city of around 100,000 inhabitants, is the most important tourist destination in Laos—a country known for its "laid back" and friendly people. It can be described as a tourist "mecca." The main road in Luang Prabang is Sisavangvong/Sakkaline Road in "the old city" tourist area. Another important street is Manthatoulat, which runs along the Mekong River. On Siasavangvong Road one finds many restaurants, tourism agencies, and massage parlors.

There are only a few tourist "sight-seeing" things to do in Luang Prabang: take a river boat for an hour and a half to a cave full of statues of Buddha, take a bus or tuk-tuk to a lovely waterfall area about an hour away from Luang Prabang, climb Phousi Hill, visit the numerous wats (the temple compounds where the monks live), and visit the Royal Palace National Museum. There is a morning market, where the inhabitants of Luang Prabang buy vegetables and other food, and there is an evening handicrafts market that stretches for many blocks along Sisavangvong Road and has wonderful fabrics and souvenirs of all kinds. Perhaps the most important tourist attraction in Luang Prabang takes place at 6:00 AM when the orange robed monks go out with their bowls to get food from the inhabitants of Luang Prabang—and have their pictures taken by tourists who get up early in the morning because they cannot resist such a wonderful photo opportunity. At 6:00 AM we can say the sacred and the profane meet in Luang Prabang.

Because the old city is so pleasant, tourists pass the time enjoying a cup of coffee or tea in the coffee shops, looking at the markets, having massages (the Lao massage is very popular; it is, at times, very painful but in a strange way, delightful), and relaxing. Luang Prabang helps people decompress and enjoy themselves. What tourists to Luang Prabang do not realize is that the Old City area of Luang Prabang was shaped by the tourist authorities in Laos, who wanted to create an area that would attract and please tourists. And it has been spectacularly successful in doing so. I asked a friend of mine who took a thirty day upscale trip through Southeast Asia what was her favorite city during her trip. "Luang Prabang," she said. "It's fabulous."

Erasure and Global Tourism in Luang Prabang

A book by architects Lynne M. Dearborn and John C. Stallmeyer, *Inconvenient Heritage: Erasure and Global Tourism in Luang Prabang,* describes the way Laotian tourism authorities shaped Luang Prabang. The book describes how the tourist area in Luang Prabang was created to please foreign tourists. To do this, certain buildings were torn down and others were remodeled to create the Luang Prabang that tourists would find appealing. What was destroyed were the buildings that authorities thought unattractive. In a sense, then, we can see Luang Prabang as a kind of Laotian Disneyland, created for tourists with the aesthetics of global tourism in mind. But the authorities had something quite splendid to begin with, and Luang Prabang does not seem artificial.

As the authors explain (2010:28):

> The designation and maintenance of many cities inscribed on the World Heritage list, including Luang Prabang, rely on the erasure of particular pasts or inconvenient heritages that are seen as potentially divisive to the local populations, unpalatable for tourists, incongruent with contemporary developments, or that do not serve the political needs of the state party's government. These erasures take place at both the physical and socio-cultural realms....A particular interpretation of Luang Prabang's cultural significance and history by the UNESCO World Heritage Committee in 1995 celebrates the city's "successful fusion of the traditional [Laotian] architectural and urban structures and those of the European colonial rulers of the nineteenth and twentieth centuries... [with a] unique townscape...remarkably well preserved, illustrating a key stage in the blending of two distinct cultural traditions."

This analysis, the authors suggest, romanticizes the French colonial occupation of Laos and pays little attention to the city's history. What tourists get, in Luang Prabang, is a highly sanitized and artificially constructed tourist mecca.

Not all of Luang Prabang is as pleasant at the tourist area. A person I met in the tourism industry in Laos gave me the name and phone number of a friend of his. "Her name is Sarah Moya. She manages a hotel in Luang Prabang. Give her a call," he said. "She'll tell you a lot about the tourism industry and probably invite you for lunch." One morning I called her, and she invited us to meet her at her hotel. I thought it was one of the many hotels in the tourism district of Luang Prabang but discovered we needed to take a tuk-tuk to get to her hotel. It was in the stadium area of Luang Prabang, on a hill overlooking the stadium. There were games going on at the stadium, so our tuk-tuk driver had to let us off near the stadium, and we wandered around for about a mile before we got to the hotel. We got to see other parts of Luang Prabang that were nice but not as refined as the tourist area. By the time we arrived in the hotel, it was lunch time, and sure enough, she invited us for lunch.

It turns out that she is the manager of the Shinta Mani hotel—a beautiful and very upscale hotel that opened in March 2011. Shinta Mani means "good heart" in Sanskrit. The hotel is, it turns out, only a ten minute drive from the tourism area of Luang Prabang, and the hotel has a free shuttle service for its patrons. We had a long and wonderful lunch at the hotel, and she told us about her career in the tourism industry. She is, as one might expect, a charming and very accomplished woman.

Her specialty, it turns out, is spending a year or two managing hotels when they open. Getting a hotel launched correctly is very important—especially when the hotel charges more than six hundred dollars a night for its best rooms. She had managed the opening of the first Shinta Mani hotel in Siem Reap and then came to Luang Prabang. She told us that she had a staff of 117 people and that it was very difficult getting good people to work at the hotel, since there were so many other opportunities for work in Luang Prabang and because many Laotians considered work as staff in hotels to be demeaning. She was kind enough to have the shuttle take us back to Luang Prabang when we'd finished our lunch.

Luang Prabang may have been "designed," so to speak, by tourism authorities, but the fact that there are so many tourists in the city and that they all seem to be delighted with it suggests that the authorities who tailored Luang Prabang for tourists did an excellent job. There are very few places that large numbers of tourists visit that have not been, to some degree, fixed up— by either by the government or private companies (or in some cases both) to make them more hospitable for tourists.

Unless tourists visited Luang Prabang many years ago, before it was recreated as a heritage tourist attraction, they would not recognize what has been done to the city. What tourists to Luang Prabang get now is the "erased" or reconstituted Luang Prabang—specially designed to appeal to tourists. Tourists, generally speaking, are most interested in pleasure, and so the reconstituted Luang Prabang most likely has more appeal to them then the "real" Luang Prabang that existed before the erasures.

Luang Prabang can accommodate all kinds of tourists—cultural tourists, world heritage tourists, group tourists, individual tourists, psychocentric tourists, and any other kind of tourist because it has accommodations at every level, from twenty dollars a night to seven hundred dollars a night, and because food and tourist attractions are relatively inexpensive.

Because it is such a pleasant place to visit, it attracts tourists from all over the world and is now one of the "must-see" cities in Southeast Asia. In 1995, before it became an UNESCO World Heritage city, it is estimated that only a few thousand tourists visited Luang Prabang.

An article by Rory Byne, "Tourism Threatens Historic City Known as 'Soul' of Laos," that appeared on a Lonely Planet internet site explains the problem Luang Prabang faced:

> Nestled deep in a Mekong River valley, Luang Prabang was cut-off from the outside world by decades of war and political isolation. A fusion of traditional Lao dwellings, French colonial architecture and more than 30 monasteries, the whole town was declared a World Heritage Site by UNESCO in 1995. The United Nations agency described it as "the best preserved city of Southeast Asia." That put Luang Prabang on the tourist map and since then the number of visitors to the town has soared from just a few thousand in 1995 to over 300,000 today.
>
> With property prices rising on the back of the tourist influx, many local people sold their properties to outside developers who turned them into internet cafes, restaurants and guesthouses. But while tourism is generating income and jobs, some residents are worried that the town is in danger of losing its identity. (www.lonelyplanet.com/thorntree/thread.jspa?threadID=1742726)

Now, that figure is more than 300,000 tourists a year and growing. But as tourism increases, the question arises—has Luang Prabang lost its soul?

Instantly hailed as the most important structure of its time, Frank Gehry's Guggenheim Museum Bilbao has celebrated more than a decade of extraordinary success. With over a hundred exhibitions and more than ten million visitors to its credit, the Guggenheim Museum Bilbao has changed the way people think about museums, and it continues to challenge assumptions about the connections between art, architecture, and collecting.

www.guggenheim.com

One of the world's most famous buildings, this museum is in many ways an attractive and impressive piece of architecture. Unfortunately, as a public space it is extremely unsuccessful—even dangerous. A spectacularly beautiful and sculptural building, the Guggenheim Bilbao succeeds monumentally in its efforts as an iconic building, and has drawn much attention to the city of Bilbao. However, the project fails miserably as a public space, missing a significant opportunity to celebrate and support the cultural and community life that is pulsating throughout the city. Situated prominently on the waterfront near the center of Bilbao, the building interrupts the life of the city, and is an insult to pedestrians who would like to use the space for anything other than gawking at the building. Frank Gehry, the architect who designed the museum, appears afraid to support, or even acknowledge, human activity in and around his buildings. The museum may bring people to Bilbao, but it only degrades the civic and cultural life that makes people proud to live in the city. Moreover, as a symbol of successful investment in architecture, it is limiting the role of architecture to mere icon.

Ethan Kent, www.pps.org/great_public_spaces/one?public_place_id=827

Chapter 12

The Guggenheim Museum, Bilbao, Spain

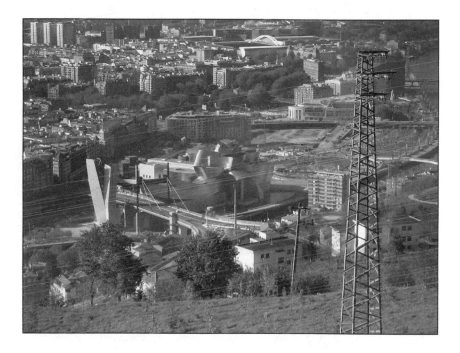

Frank Gehry, the Canadian-American architect who created the Guggenheim Museum in Bilbao in 1998, did two things with this museum: first, he designed the most talked-about building of recent years, and second, he put Bilbao on the tourist map. The building was part of Bilbao's master plan to develop tourism in the city, and the Guggenheim museum was, it would seem, wildly successful on that front.

Gehry describes how he arrived at the design of the building. In an article on his work by Matt Tyrnauer, "Architecture in the Age of Gehry," which appeared in *Vanity Fair,* we read:

> "Overall, the kind of language I've developed, which culminated in Bilbao, comes from a reaction to Postmodernism. I was desperate not to go there,"

Gehry explains, in his refreshingly plainspoken style. "I was looking for a way to deal with the humanizing qualities of decoration without doing it. I got angry with it—all the historical stuff, the pastiche. I said to myself, If you have to go backward, why not go back 300 million years before man, to fish? And that's when I started with this fish shtick, as I think of it, and started drawing the damn things, and I realized that they were architectural, conveying motion even when they were not moving. I don't like to portray it to other people as a complicated intellectual endeavor. Most architects avoid double curves, as I did, because we didn't have a language for translation into a building that was viable and economical. I think the study of fish allowed me to create a kind of personal language… Well, that goddamn fish, when you stood beside it, felt like it moved…I realized that by accident I had found it. And so the next move was to cut off the tail, get rid of all the kitsch things, and see how much you could take away, go to a more minimal look."

So his design represented a reaction to what Gehry regarded as the excesses, in architecture, of both modernism and postmodernism, and an attempt to come up with something different. The general public now seems to find modernist buildings, with their slabs of steel, glass and concrete, cold and alienating, and postmodernist buildings, which combine many architectural genres (visual eclecticism), amusing and a pleasant break from modernist structures.

Modernism and Postmodernism

Literally speaking, the term postmodernism (also known as "pomo") means "coming after" modernism. The term "post" means "after," but it can also mean "moving beyond," "different from," or "the opposite of." What we call the modernist period, culture theorists suggest, dominated our cultural life between 1900 and 1960. The postmodernist period, then, involves the years from 1960 to the present. Postmodernist thinkers believe that there was a sudden "cultural mutation" around 1960 and that this mutation, this remarkable change in beliefs, attitudes, philosophies, and aesthetic sensibilities is what is explained by postmodernism. It replaced modernism in our arts, architecture, literature, and other aspects of culture. This mutation led to a new kind of tourist as well—the postmodernist tourist interested in pleasure and entertainment and not in authenticity.

12. *The Guggenheim Museum, Bilbao, Spain*

A French scholar, Jean-François Lyotard, writing in *The Postmodern Condition: A Report on Knowledge*, explains postmodernism as follows:

> Simplifying to the extreme, I define *postmodern* as incredulity toward metanarratives. This incredulity is undoubtedly a product of progress in the sciences: but that progress in turn presupposes it. To the obsolescence of the metanarrative apparatus of legitimation corresponds, most notably, the crisis of metaphysical philosophy and of the university institution which in the past relied on it. The narrative function is losing its functors, its great hero, its great dangers, its great voyages, its great goal. (1984:xxiv)

This somewhat elliptical statement, in which Lyotard defines postmodernism as involving "incredulity toward metanarratives" is probably the most famous definition of the term ever written. We no longer have faith, Lyotard argues, in the great all-encompassing, wide-ranging supernarratives—the systems of thought (as expounded in religions, political ideologies, and philosophy) that have grounded us in the past. Instead, in a postmodern world, we have many different narratives vying for our attention, which has led to a crisis of legitimation. Who has the answers? Whose beliefs are valid? What's right and wrong?

We must contrast postmodernism with the modernism that preceded it. The term "modern" comes from the fifth-century Latin word *modernus,* which was used to differentiate the pagan era from the Christian era. Postmodernism develops at the same time that consumer capitalism becomes dominant, and thus postmodernism is associated with consumer culture and the mass consumption that dominates fashion and shapes people's lifestyles. We live now in a world dominated by media and images and simulations of reality; this world of signs and simulations has undermined our sense of reality and dissolved our sense that there are fixed structures and stable boundaries, that anything has meaning. Like so many belief systems, postmodernism is intimately connected to the system it rejected and replaced—modernism.

Let me summarize now some of the differences between postmodernism and modernism that have been mentioned or implied in the discussion above. First, if modernism involves differentiation (between the elite arts and popular culture), postmodernism involves what can be described as de-differentiation, breaking down the barriers between the elite arts and popular culture and reveling joyfully in mass culture. If modernism involves a "high seriousness" towards life, postmodernism involves an element of game playing and an ironic stance as well as a kind of play-fulness. In postmodernist societies, people "play" with their identities, changing them when they feel bored with their old ones.

If modernism involves stylistic purity, as reflected visually in modern-ist architecture, postmodernism involves stylistic eclecticism and variety, with the pastiche as the governing metaphor. If modernism believes we can know reality, postmodernism argues that we are all confounded by illusions and what the French sociologist Jean Baudrillard called "hyper-reality," as exemplified in Disneyland. Postmodernism is the realm of con-sumer culture, in contrast to what we might call the production culture of modernism. An increasingly important part of contemporary consumer culture involves tourism. Tourism, we must remember, is a form of con-sumption, but of experiences rather than goods. The heroes of modernism are the great businessmen and statesmen, while the heroes of postmod-ernism tend to be celebrities and entertainment figures, whose tastes and consumption habits are held up as models to us all.

If postmodern theory were some interesting notion that philosophers debated about, but that had little or no impact on our everyday lives, it probably wouldn't have achieved the notoriety it has gained. The argu-ment of postmodernist theorists is that postmodernism has profoundly affected many aspects of our societies and our lives, whether or not we are aware of this being so. In our case, the postmodernization of society has led to the postmodernization of tourism.

In his book *After the Great Divide: Modernism, Mass Culture, Postmodernism*, Andreas Huyssen writes that it is in architecture that we see, most clearly, how postmodernism has broken away from modernism. He offers the example of the great modernist Dutch architect Mies van der Rohe, whose "glass curtain walls" differ profoundly from the work of postmodern architects, with their use of mixed styles. Thus, he cites, as a typical postmodern building, Philip Johnson's famous AT&T skyscraper, which has Roman colonnades at its street level, a neoclassical midsection, and a Chippendale pediment at its top. And now, the most famous post-modern building (though Gehry asserts his building is not postmodern) is Gehry's Guggenheim Museum in Bilbao.

Christopher Jencks, an architect who has written extensively on post-modernism architecture, offers an interesting perspective on the topic:

> Modern architecture had failed to remain credible partly because it
> didn't communicate with its ultimate users—the main argument of my

book, *The Language of Post-Modern Architecture*—and partly because it didn't make effective links with the city and history. Thus the solution I perceived and defined as postmodern: an architecture that was professionally based and popular as well as one that was based on new techniques and old patterns. Double coding, to simplify, means both elite/popular culture and new/old, and there are compelling reasons for these opposite pairings. Today's postmodern architects were trained by modernists, and are committed to using contemporary technology as well as facing current social reality. These commitments are enough to distinguish them from revivalists or traditionalists, a point worth stressing since it creates their hybrid language, the style of postmodern architecture. (1991:4–5)

Many architects were trained by modernist architects and rejected this style of architecture, but, they claimed, they didn't want to create postmodern buildings. This is true of Gehry, who was a modernist architect for a while but then rejected it—but also rejected, so he claims, postmodernism.

Gehry said he wanted to avoid postmodernism. His Bilbao building was, as he put it, "a reaction to postmodernism. I didn't want to go there." He may have created what we can describe as a post-postmodern building. It is extremely difficult to describe the Guggenheim Museum. Like many of Gehry's buildings, it can perhaps best be described as looking like a crumpled piece of paper turned into a building. The dilemma he faced as an architect involved deciding where to go, stylistically. He became interested in abstract forms and in the design possibilities of fish, which he believed conveyed motion even when the fish weren't moving. Once he decided on a building that looked something like a fish cut into different sections, he needed to employ advanced computer programs, used to build fighter jets, to design the building, because it has forms that are extremely difficult to construct. Since Gehry is computer illiterate, he had his associates in his office use the program.

J. G. Ballard, in his article "The Larval Stage of a New Kind of Architecture" (2007), suggests that the building doesn't fit into any of our conventional categories for understanding a building:

I wonder if the Bilbao Guggenheim is a work of architecture at all? Perhaps it belongs to the category of exhibition and fairground displays, of giant inflatables and bouncy castles. The Guggenheim may be the first permanent temporary structure. Its interior is a huge disappointment, nd confirms the suspicion that the museum is a glorified sales aid for the Guggenheim brand. There is a giant atrium, always a sign that some corporation's hand is sliding towards your wallet, but the galleries are conventionally proportioned, and one can't help feeling that they are irrelevant anyway. The museum is its own work of art, and the only one really on display.... Architecture today is a visitor attraction, deliberately playing on our love of the brightest lights and the gaudiest neon. The Bilbao Guggenheim's spiritual Acropolis is Las Vegas, with its infantilising pirate ships and Egyptian sphinxes. Gehry's museum would be completely at home there, for a year at least, and then look a little dusty and jaded, soon to be torn down and replaced by another engaging marvel with which our imaginations can play.

Ballard's critique may supply the answer to the enigma that Gehry's Guggenheim Museum present to us—we don't know how to categorize it, and without being able to classify it as modern or postmodern, we become confused. The museum may be an example of post-postmodern architecture, though nobody knows what the term post-postmodern might mean. Whatever kind of building it might be, if it is a building, and despite its faults—and what building doesn't have faults—it succeeded in astonishing the world and putting a rather seedy, out of the way, second-rate city, Bilbao, on the tourism map. It also turned the world of architecture upside down, freed architecture from "the box," and made it possible for architects to design buildings, or non-buildings or anti-buildings, that never would have been considered before it was built.

The remarkable design of the building and its notoriety caught the attention of the tourism media apparatus, tourism companies, and tourists. Matthew Arnold, a British literary theorist, once talked about our becoming familiar with "the best that has been thought and said." Tourists, we may say, search for the best that has been built. Forbes magazine, for example, had an article about the Gehry museum and what it described as "the Bilbao Effect" (www.forbes.com/2002/02/20/0220conn.html).

As Martin Bailey explained (for *The Art Newspaper*):

> With its dramatic architecture, the museum continues to be a major draw, attracting people who would otherwise not come. The Bilbao estimates that its economic impact on the local economy was worth €168 million (approximately $147 million) last year—up from €149 million ($130 million) in 2000—and it also brought in a further €27 million ($23 million) to the Basque treasury in taxes. This represents the equivalent of

4,415 jobs. A visitor survey revealed that 82% came to the city of Bilbao exclusively to see the museum or had extended their stay in the city to visit it.

We see, then, that it is the museum that attracts most tourists to Bilbao. A study made by the city of Bilbao offers added evidence of the impact of the Gehry museum on tourism in Bilbao:

> Several studies attempt to evaluate the effects of the tourist sector which received a strong boost from the inauguration of the Guggenheim Museum in 1997 (e.g. Rodríguez *et al*, 2001; González, 2006; Plaza, 2007). Opinions about the so-called 'Guggenheim effect' on Bilbao's and the region's economy are however divided. From one perspective, it is a fact that tourism in Bilbao has increased sharply. There was also a big increase in airport passengers from 1.4 million in 1994 to 3.8 million in 2005 (Bilbao Ayuntamiento, 2007; Lan Ekintza, 2007). Bilbao now receives more tourists than San Sebastian, traditionally the leading Basque tourist destination. The Guggenheim alone has attracted an average of 1 million visitors per year since its opening (Plaza, 2007). Some voices criticize the large amounts of public money that went into the building of the museum and the public subsidies that are required to finance its liabilities. (eprints.lse.ac.uk/3624/1/Bilbao_city_report_(final).pdf)

The Gehry Bilbao museum has now become an important destination for cultural tourists, who are interested in visiting great monuments and buildings and now find it worth visiting Bilbao, a relatively uninteresting city from a tourist's perspective, to do so.

Theorizing Tourism: Analyzing Iconic Destinations by Arthur Asa Berger, 112–119.

As the most famous of the Mayan pyramids on the Yucatán peninsula, Chichén Itzá has been studied extensively and is the most popular Mayan ruin in México. Much has been written about it.. .. The main attraction is the central pyramid, also known as El Castillo, this spectacular, massive Mesoamerican step-pyramid that dominates the Chichen Itza archaeological site in the Mexican state of Yucatan. Today El Castillo is one of the most popular and recognized tourist sites of Mexico and as of 07/07/07, it is one of the Seven New Wonders of the World. Built by the Maya sometime between 1000 and 1200 AD, El Castillo served as a temple to the god Kukulkan and is believed to have served as a calendar. Each of the structure's four stairways contains 91 steps. When counting the top platform as another step, in total El Castillo has 365 steps, one step for each day of the year. The structure is 24 meters tall (78 feet), plus an additional 6 m (20 feet) for the temple top, for a total height of 30 meters (98 feet). The square base measures 55.3 meters (181 feet) across. Huge sculptures of plumed serpent's heads sit at the base of the pyramid on the northern staircase. At sunset during the spring and autumn equinoxes triangle shadows are formed by the platforms making it appear as if a plumed serpent is descending the pyramid.

yucatantoday.com/en/topics/chichen-itza

Chapter 13

Chichen Itza, Mexico

Chichen Itza, which means, according to some translations, "at the mouth of the well of Itza," is one of the most famous Mayan tourist sites in the Yucatan peninsula in Mexico. The giant Pyramid of Kukulkan or El Castillo, a temple and pyramid devoted to the Mayan god Kukulkan, is the central attraction of the site, which also features a Temple of the Warriors, a Temple of the Jaguar, a Great Ball court, a Cenote of Sacrifice, a nunnery complex, and an astrological observatory, El Caracol. In other words, Chichen Itza is a large site with many buildings. When I visited Chichen Itza, it was possible to climb to the tops of the Great Pyramid and the Temple of the Warriors, but since January 2006, this is no long possible.

The site attracts around 3 million visitors a year and thus is one of the most popular tourist sites in Mexico.

Tourists generally do not know anything about the economic and political aspects of the sites they visit. Chichen Itza is often described, in academic archaeological and tourism literature, as a site where native peoples have been marginalized and government and the tourism industry have appropriated a site that really belonged to the Mayan people. In an article, "Tourism in the Mundo Maya: Inventions and (Mis)Representations of Maya Identities and Heritage," Aline Magnoni, Traci Ardren, and Scott Hutson deal with this matter in some detail. They write:

> Today's Maya people live in modern nation states where they relate, generally from a marginalized position as a result of colonial domination, to other local and transnational social groups (van den Berghe 1995). Moreover, the popular depiction of "the living Maya as keepers of timeless cultural heritage" fails to mention the historical and modern conditions of poverty and oppression that have contributed to the maintenance of traditions and conservative practices (Pyburn 1998:124). These notions of continuity draw on essentialized and exoticized interpretations of past and present Maya that fulfill Western fantasies instead of focusing on the complex processes of cultural and historical change that social groups undergo through time. (2007:353–383)

What we find, then, is that while tourists have little idea of the nature of the struggles that have gone on at contemporary Chichen Itza (and many other important tourism sites), scholars in a variety of disciplines have documented the conflicts that often occur in such sites.

These tourism wars are described by an anthropologist, Quetzil E. Castaneda, in his article "Tourism 'Wars' in the Yucatan" as follows:

> On New Year's Eve 2004 I returned to Pisté, Yucatán, México, where I have been doing ethnographic research since 1985. Some close friends were anxious to fill me in on the latest and most important gossip: the *artesanos* (artisans) had *reinvadieron* (re-invaded) the archaeological zone of the famous ancient Maya city and tourist destination of Chichén Itzá.
>
> The invasion (the local term for the illegal presence) of handicraft producers and vendors selling inside *la zona*, or the legally defined archaeological zone, has a long history. It is the third invasion that can be traced to an ongoing 23-year-old problem. Since 1983, in response to an increased flow of tourists related to the emergence of Cancun resorts in the late 1970s, there has been a meteoric rise of participation in the informal sector of handicraft production and petty entrepreneurship in

Pisté, only 3 kilometers from Chichén. From some 20 Pisté vendedores (vendors) and artisans in 1982, the number grew to 200 in 1983 to cap at 300 in 1984 up through the present. Organized in factional groups, these vendors and artisans petitioned the state and federal governments to create adequate market venues. Because these petitions were alternatively ignored or betrayed, the invasion of the heritage zone became the choice expression of their unresolved, ongoing petition—interpellation—of the government to respond to the needs of the community—to act as *good* government. (www.aaanet.org/press/an/infocus/Heritage_In_Focus/Castaneda.htm)

What tourists to Chichen Itza don't realize, then, is that it is the site of a prolonged battle between the wealthy family that owns the land and indigenous Maya peoples who live in the area or who have come to the site from outside the area—and want to sell handicrafts, and to work in the site as administrators.

Castaneda describes what led to the problem at Chichen Itza. It turns out that the National Institute of Anthropology and History (INAH) had twenty employees who lived and worked inside the site as wardens, from 1923 until 1983. They had a monopoly on the sale of food and artisan products. In 1983 the government asked them to leave their homes inside the site but allowed them the right to sell things at two places inside the site in open-air buildings called palapas, disenfranchising the local people. This led, Castaneda goes on to explain, to an "invasion" of the Chichen Itzá zone:

> The crux of the problem is that these INAH heritage workers were thus given a monopoly while hundreds from the same town of Pisté were disenfranchised from selling inside the zone and forced to marginal locations. In protest of this monopoly and in petition of the government to create adequate marketing venues for them, *vendedores* and *artesanos* invaded the zone. Further, the archaeological zone, while legally defined as heritage, the *land* of heritage is owned as both communal property by Pisté *ejidatarios* under Mexican *ejido* law and as private property by the Barbachano family, one of the most powerful of Yucatán's oligarchy. Only the ruins per se—piles of carved rocks, shards, fragments of paint, and stone chips—*on top of the land* are *patrimonio cultural* (federally-owned heritage). These ambiguities began to be exploited by the Barbachano's in the latter 1990s with covert tactics that ultimately led to the expulsion of the INAH *custodios* from the *palapas* and their complete

takeover by the Barbachanos at the end of 2004. Once again in protest of the monopoly sale of tourist products inside the zone and nine years after the last invasion, the *vendedores* re-entered *la zona*.

We can see Chichen Itza not only as a fantastic, world-class archaeological site, where ball games in the ball court led to the beheading of the captain of the losing team—a great honor for those involved—but also as a site that has been contested over the years by indigenous people and outside forces, such as the government and the owner of the site. There is money to be made at world-class tourism sites, and it is not unusual for "wars" to take place between competing interests. Generally speaking, it is the indigenous people who live at these sites who lose these wars.

We should recognize that this site is a signifier of the Maya heritage of Central America. In addition to tourist souvenir dollars, entry fees, tour fares, and hotel income all go to the government of Mexico (based in far away Mexico City) or to international corporations, not to the Maya whose heritage the site is displaying.

Another site that has been contested by indigenous people is the Lords of Sipan Museum in Lambayeque, Peru, which I had the pleasure of visiting recently. Its treasures are simply amazing. The museum, built with German funds, houses a treasure comparable to that of King Tutankhamen that was found near the town of Sipan in the 1970s and was supposed to be moved to the national capital Lima for display. The local people rebelled at the thought of losing this treasure, and the museum was built at the regional capital Lambayeque instead, but not at the town of Sipan, where the material was discovered. The Lords of Sipan conflict between regional peoples and the national government is yet another example of the complications that can arise when the tourism interests of a national government conflict with those of indigenous people. It is also a rare example where the local community was successful in retaining its cultural treasures, partly for community pride and partly in hopes of drawing tourism to its region.

Theorizing Tourism: Analyzing Iconic Destinations by Arthur Asa Berger, 120–125.
© 2013 Left Coast Press, Inc. All rights reserved.

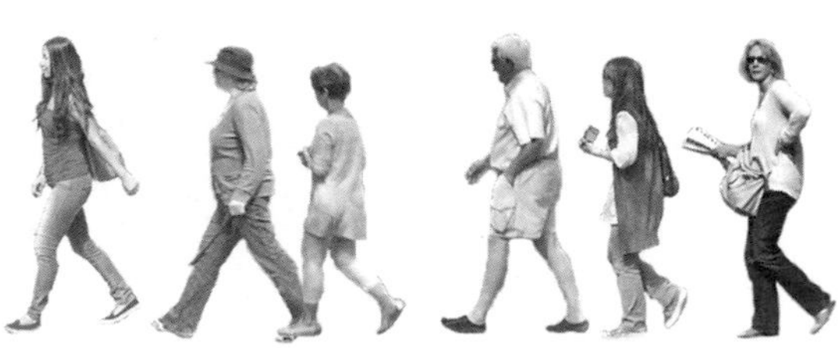

The Potala Palace symbolizes Tibetan Buddhism and its central role in the traditional administration of Tibet....Construction of the Potala Palace began at the time of Songtsen of the Thubet (Tubo) dynasty in the 7th century AD. It was rebuilt in the mid-17th century by the 5th Dalai Lama in a campaign that lasted 30 years, reaching its present size in the years that followed, as a result of repeated renovation and expansion. The Potala is located on Red Mountain, 3,700 m above sea level, in the centre of the Lhasa valley. It covers an area of over 130,000 m² and stands more than 110 m high. The White palace is approached by a winding road leading to an open square in front of the palace. Its central section is the East Main Hall, where all the main ceremonies take place. The throne of the Dalai Lama is on the north side of the hall, the walls of which are covered with paintings depicting religious and historical themes. At the top of the White Palace is the personal suite of the Dalai Lama. The Red Palace lies to the west of the White Palace. Its purpose is to house the stupas holding the remains of the Dalai Lamas. It also contains many Buddha and sutra halls. To the west of the Red Palace is the Namgyel Dratshang, the private monastery of the Dalai Lama. Other important components of the Potala complex are the squares to the north and south and the massive palace walls, built from rammed earth and stone and pierced by gates on the east, south and west sides.

whc.unesco.org/en/list/707

The Potala Palace, covering a total area of 36 thousand square meters with the elevation of over 3700 meters, is the highest and largest palace-style complex in the world. The main building of the Potala Palace is 117 meters high with actually 9 layers consisting of White House and Red House. The whole complex has over ten thousand pillars. Inside the Potala Palace there are many religious symbols, antiques, colorful murals depicting different scenes associated with Buddhism and the history of Tibet showing the relation between Tibetan government and the central state of Ming and Qing Dynasties in the past. The Potala Palace is attracting more and more travelers and pilgrims from all over the world. To protect the palace, the palace only accepts 2300 visitors every day.

www.itourschina.com/travelguide/the-potala-palace.htm

Chapter 14

Potala Palace, Lhasa, Tibet

Tibet was invaded by the People's Liberation Army in 1951 and annexed as part of China. In 1959 the Dalai Lama and 80,000 Tibetans fled to India, where the Tibetan people set up a government in exile in Dharamsala. But no governments recognize this government in exile, and the Dalai Lama has not been successful in convincing the Chinese government to offer Tibetans autonomy under Chinese rule. The Chinese government embarked on a so-called Tibetan liberalization and modernization policy in 1980, but tensions between the Chinese authorities and the Tibetan people have always been great, and there have been a number of violent Tibetan rebellions over the years. The Chinese government has induced many Han Chinese to settle in Tibet, and now there are half as many Chinese in the Tibetan plateau as Tibetans. This represents an attempt to overwhelm Tibetan culture by bringing so many Chinese into the country, but this move has exacerbated the problem between China and the Tibetan people, who see their culture in danger of being destroyed.

In 1959, after the Dalai Lama fled Tibet, the Chinese government turned the Potala Palace—for more than a thousand years the seat of Tibetan Buddhism—into a museum, and so it now functions as a tourist attraction. We must remember that Tibet was a theocracy, and the Dalai Lama was not only the spiritual leader of the Tibetan people, but also their political leader. Not only is the Potala Palace a masterpiece of Tibetan architecture, it also contains many works of art, relics, and artifacts of interest to cultural tourists. It is a stone and wood structure that contains more than 1,000 rooms. In the Potala Palace there are chanting halls, temples, stupas housing the remains of earlier Dalai Lamas, and many thousands of statues of the Buddha.

The Potala Palace also stands as a symbol of the conflict that has gone on for many years between the Tibetan people and China since the People's Republic of China took control of (some would say invaded and occupied) Tibet. China built a railroad to Tibet, an incredible feat of engineering, and now traffic between Tibet and other parts of China has increased considerably. It was Tibet's remoteness that allowed it to develop its culture the way it did, but that changed when modern means of transportation made the country much more accessible.

We can see this problem as described in an article on "Tourism Development and Cultural Policies in China" by Trevor Sofield and Sarah Li that appeared in an issue of *Annals of Tourism:*

> In 1989, China commenced a five-year-long restoration of the Potala Palace in Lhasa, the former residence of the Dalai Lama, in an attempt to demonstrate its concern for, and preservation of, minority cultures. It was opened as a heritage museum in August 1994 in a celebration coinciding with the Shoton, the annual Tibetan harvest festival. Hailed by the Chinese as evidence of their genuine regard for ethnic cultures, the opening drew fierce criticism from the exiled Dalai Lama. Lodi Gyari, a principal adviser to the Dalai Lama and president of the International Campaign for Tibet, was quoted as saying that the Chinese had turned the Potala Palace into a monument of a vanquished people: "Our most sacred palace will become nothing more than a mere showpiece of tourism for Chinese package tours. For Tibetans it's just another example of the death of our culture" (Hong Kong *Sunday Morning Post*, 7 August 1994). (1998:375)

Turning the Potala Palace into a "museum" reflects, it could be suggested, an attempt by Chinese authorities to place Tibetan Buddhism in the category of dead religions, and, to make things worse, to use it to make money from tourists. Being a tourist in Tibet used to be a rarity, since it was so difficult to get there and be allowed to visit the country. Now, with the railroad, a visit to Tibet has lost its uniqueness. Tibet is a good case study of Plog's typology. At first only allocentric adventurers visited the country. As the Chinese authorities developed tourism in Tibet, more and more people visited the country—by plane. Now, although its extreme height can be a problem, thanks to the railroad, even the most psychocentric tourists can visit Tibet, generally in group tours. Visiting Tibet can be seen as a combination of cultural tourism, heritage tourism, and "soft" adventure tourism.

Until the 1950s, it was extremely difficult to gain entrance to Tibet and all that people in Western countries knew about it came from books by writers who somehow managed to sneak into the country. One of the most important sources of information about Tibet in the '50s was Heinrich Harrer's *Seven Years in Tibet,* first published in 1953. There were other books that were similar in nature, describing a "hidden" and mysterious Tibet. One of the most popular was T. Lobsang Rama's *The Third Eye: The Autobiography of a Tibetan Lama,* which was published in 1956, a book that I read and found fascinating. It was discovered later that the book was a literary hoax, written by an Irishman named Cyril Hoskins, who was a plumber's son.

Now, things have changed considerably. As John Powers explains in his book *Introduction to Tibetan Buddhism,* as a result of the annexation of Tibet by the People's Republic of China, and the exiling of the Dalai Lama and many other Tibetan lamas, we now know a great deal more about Tibet and Tibetan Buddhism. He writes (2007:12):

> The tragedy of Tibet's invasion and annexation by the People's Republic of China in the 1950s has had a devastating effect on the people of Tibet and their rich traditional culture, but the rest of the world has benefited from the resulting Diaspora, which has brought Tibetan lamas out of their monasteries and retreat huts and into universities and newly-established Buddhist centers. Now students can have access to them in ways that would have been impossible in traditional Tibet. As a result of their exposure to teachings and teachers from this tradition, thousands of Westerners have become Tibetan Buddhists, and there is widespread interest even among nonconverts in the public lectures of such luminaries as the Dalai Lama, Sogyel Rinpoche, Perna Norbu Rinpoche, and Sakya Tridzin. Modern technology allows their words to be printed and disseminated all over the world, in print and electronic forms.

The irony of the Chinese annexation of Tibet and the Dalai Lama's fleeing the country is that Tibetan Buddhism is now much more a part of world culture.

The Potala Palace, without the Dalai Lama in residence and with only a small number of monks living there, stands as a symbol of the repression of the Tibetan people by the People's Republic of China and its attempt, many would argue, to destroy Tibetan Buddhism and Tibetan culture. Some tourists refuse to visit Tibet because of the repressive actions of the Chinese government, but others, lured by the possibility of visiting such a remote and remarkable country and the relative ease of doing so, put politics aside. This is not unusual. Tourists often visit countries with repressive political regimes since the repression doesn't affect them and because they think (and this is probably a rationalization) that tourism will have a positive impact on the politics of the country and help lessen repression. Thus, people visited Spain during the Franco years and visit other countries where the people are oppressed. Tourists, generally speaking, don't experience the political repression that the people in the countries they visit feel.

In recent years, a number of Tibetan monks and nuns have set themselves on fire to call attention to the way Chinese authorities are attacking Tibetan monks and the general populace and systematically trying to destroy the religious, cultural, and linguistic identity of people in Tibet. Maria Ontero, an under secretary for civilian security, democracy and human rights and U.S. Special Coordinator for Tibetan Issues sent a letter to the Chinese government on January 24, 2012, criticizing Chinese policies in Tibet and stating, in part:

> These policies include dramatically expanded Chinese government controls on religious life and practice; ongoing "patriotic education" campaigns within monasteries that require monks to denounce the Dalai Lama; the permanent placement of Chinese officials in monasteries; increasingly intensive surveillance, arbitrary detentions and disappearances of Tibetans; and restrictions on and imprisonment of some families and friends of self-immolators. Over the last year, Chinese government security and judicial officials also have detained and imprisoned Tibetan writers, artists, intellectuals, and cultural advocates who criticized Chinese government policies.

The matter is complicated because most countries accept the Chinese government's assertion that Tibet has always been a province of China. It was neglected by China because of its remoteness, but that has changed since the 1950s. India recognized Tibet as being a semi-autonomous region of China a number of years ago, giving credence to China's claim over Tibet.

There is a story titled the "Banyan: The Buddha and the tigress" that appeared in the *Economist* (March 10, 2012) that offers another insight into the Tibetan-Chinese relationship. It tells the story of how the Buddha took pity on a starving Chinese tigress and sacrificed himself to her so she didn't have to eat her newborn cubs. The moral of the story is that Buddhism abhors violence but allows it for the greater good. The article pointed out that in the prior year, twenty-six Tibetans had immolated themselves and that in the month of March, 2012, more Tibetans immolated themselves. None of these immolations changed the policies of the Chinese government, and they may even have been counter-productive and led to more repression in Tibet.

The irony of the situation is that it would seem that China is making a big mistake in not making an accommodation with the Dalai Lama, since only the Dalai Lama can make Tibetans accept Chinese rule. The fact that the Potala Palace has been turned into a museum can be seen, then, as a signifier of the repression of the Tibetan people and of the attempt by Chinese authorities to suppress Tibetan religion and culture and, sadly, a lost opportunity by the Chinese authorities to bring peace to Tibet. As things stand now, the Chinese government is focused on maintaining control of Tibet, exploiting its mineral wealth and its draw as an important tourist destination.

Tibet is yet another example of the phenomenon we saw in Chichen Itza, when a remote government attempts to assert its authority against the wishes of the indigenous people. In both Tibet and Chichen Itza, there is an ongoing battle between the government and the people living in the site or, in the case of Tibet, conflict about power and the control of touristic sites and everyday life. Unfortunately for the Tibetan people, China is not likely to ease the repression there, and the possibilities for continued violence remain strong.

Theorizing Tourism: Analyzing Iconic Destinations by Arthur Asa Berger, 126–131.

Masada today is one of the Jewish people's greatest symbols. Israeli soldiers take an oath there: "Masada shall not fall again." Next to Jerusalem, it is the most popular destination of Jewish tourists visiting Israel. It is strange that a place known only because 960 Jews committed suicide there in the first century C.E. should become a modern symbol of Jewish survival. What is even stranger is that the Masada episode is not mentioned in the Talmud. Why did the rabbis choose to ignore the courageous stance and tragic fate of the last fighters in the Jewish rebellion against Rome? After Rome destroyed Jerusalem and the Second Temple in 70, the Great Revolt ended—except for the surviving Zealots, who fled Jerusalem to the fortress of Masada, near the Dead Sea. There, they held out for three years. Anyone who has climbed the famous "snake path" to Masada can understand why the surrounding Roman troops had to content themselves with a siege. Masada is situated on top of an enormous, isolated rock: Anyone climbing it to attack the fortress would be an easy target. Yet the Jews, encamped in the fortress, could never feel secure; every morning, they awoke to see the Roman Tenth Legion hard at work, constructing battering rams and other weapons. If the 960 defenders of Masada hoped that the Romans eventually would consider this last Jewish beachhead too insignificant to bother conquering, they were to be disappointed. Once it became apparent that the Tenth Legion's battering rams and catapults would soon succeed in breaching Masada's walls, Eleazar ben Yair, the Zealots' leader, decided that all the Jewish defenders should commit suicide. Because Jewish law strictly forbids suicide, this decision sounds more shocking today than it probably did to his compatriots. The alternatives facing the fortress's defenders were hardly more attractive than death. Once the Romans defeated them, the men could expect to be sold off as slaves, the women as slaves and prostitutes.

www.jewishvirtuallibrary.org/jsource/Judaism/masada.html

Chapter 15

Masada, Israel

When I visited Israel a number of years ago, like many tourists I took a day trip to the Masada and the Dead Sea, which is nearby. Some people actually climb up the winding path that leads to the Masada, but most tourists take the cable car. Masada is perched on top of a very steep hill and is very inaccessible. I could only marvel that any army could build attack ramps that would enable it to take Masada, but that is what happened. Supposedly two women and five children hid themselves and were not killed by Eleazar's men. From them, thanks to the Roman Jewish historian Flavius Josephus, we have Eleazar's speech:

> Since we long ago my generous friends resolved never to be servants to the Romans, nor to any other than to God Himself, Who alone is the true and just Lord of mankind, the time is now come that obliges us to make that resolution true in practice.... We were the very first that revolted [against Rome], and we are the last that fight against them; and I cannot but esteem it as a favor that God has granted us, that it is still in our power to die bravely, and in a state of freedom. Let our wives die before they are abused, and our children before they have tasted of

slavery, and after we have slain them, let us bestow that glorious benefit upon one another mutually. (www.israeltour.com/categories/about/masada.asp)

According to Josephus, Eleazar had everything in Masada destroyed, except the food, since it would be "a testimonial when we are dead that we were not subdued for want of necessities; but that, according to our original resolution, we have preferred death before slavery."

The account by Josephus is the only one we have of what transpired at Masada, and there is some question about how accurate he was and to what degree he imposed his own ideas upon what happened there. An Israeli scholar, Shaye D. Cohen, wrote a book, *The Significance of Yavneh and Other Essays on Jewish Hellenism* (2010) in which he suggests that archaeological evidence casts doubt on some of the story that Josephus told. As Cohen writes in his chapter "Masada: Literary Tradition, Archaeological Evidence and the Credibility of Josephus":

> We do not know what happened at the summit of Masada on the fifteenth of Xanthicus in 74 CE. The archaeological discoveries of Professor Yadin show that Masada was besieged by the Romans in the fashion described by Josephus, but they do not tell us how the defenders of Masada were killed. (www.pbs.org/wgbh/pages/frontline/shows/religion/portrait/masada.html)

Josephus said that all the food stuffs were left, but archaeological evidence suggests that this was not the case, and there are other discrepancies between the Josephus account and the archaeological evidence.

The Tenth Legion of the Roman Army, led by Flavius Silva, breached the walls of Masada in 74 AD and found it in flames. One problem with the Masada story, as told by Josephus, is that modern archaeologists have not found the remains of 960 people. There are some scholars who believe the Masada story is a myth and that a mass suicide never took place there. Masada can be seen as a metaphor for the situation in which Israel now finds itself—surrounded by enemies, who have invaded the country many times in an attempt to destroy it; however, unlike the situation at Masada, Israel has a very powerful army and has been able to rebuff the invasions. But Israel still finds itself, like Masada, in a perilous situation with hostile enemies all around it and a never-ending need to maintain itself and its free and democratic society against hostile enemies who have vowed to destroy it.

Masada may be somewhat responsible for what we might describe as the "siege mentality" that one finds in contemporary Israel—the result of the fact that Israel is surrounded by hostile countries that are analogous, one might say, to the Roman Tenth Legion that surrounded Masada. Some psychologists also describe a phenomenon found in some Israelis that they call the "Masada Complex," which refers to the belief that death is preferable to the loss of liberty and statehood. Political scientist Susan Hattis Rolef has defined this "complex," found mostly in very conservative Israeli politicians, as "the conviction ... that it is preferable to fight to the end rather than to surrender and acquiesce to the loss of independent statehood" (*Political Dictionary of the State of Israel,* 1993:214).

Like many other traumatic historical events, Masada still plays an important role in Israeli politics and tourism in Israel. The story of Masada still lingers in the memory of Jews in Israel and in other countries where Jews are found. Unless they are in Israel, many Jewish people have anxieties about being in a small minority in the countries where they live. Masada also plays an important role in Jewish tourism since it is such a popular site for tourists. One of the most important motivations of Jewish tourists (and non-Jewish tourists as well) is "to participate in Israel's history."

Tourists want to see for themselves where some important event took place—especially an event of such consequence for Jewish history and one that has meaning for Jewish people everywhere. Visiting Masada, especially for Jewish people from countries all over the world, is a form of heritage tourism and also represents, for most tourists, a way for tourists to show their support for the state of Israel and the Israeli government. According to the Jewish Virtual Library:

> Masada today is one of the Jewish people's greatest symbols. Israeli soldiers take an oath there: "Masada shall not fall again." Next to Jerusalem, it is the most popular destination of Jewish tourists visiting Israel. As a rabbi, I have even had occasion to conduct five Bar and Bat Mitzvah services there. It is strange that a place known only because 960 Jews committed suicide there in the first century C.E. should become a modern symbol of Jewish survival. (www.jewishvirtuallibrary.org/jsource/Judaism/masada.html)

Masada, then, plays an important role in tourism in Israel and also is one of the foundations of the narratives that Jewish people tell themselves about their past. It is part of Jewish mythology. Myths, we must remember, are stories people tell about their earliest heroes.

What would happen, we may ask, if archaeological work there proved that a massacre never occurred at Masada? I would answer this question by suggesting that the evidence we have suggests that there actually was a mass suicide at Masada and that it may be impossible to prove that there wasn't one. But even if it were possible to prove that the Masada mass suicide is sheer mythology, that doesn't mean its importance to the Jewish people would be minimized. Myths, we must remember, are stories *believed to be true* about heroes and the founding of a society. Whether they are true or not, curiously, becomes of secondary significance to people who believe something and want to believe in the story of Masada, since it is so intimately connected, historically, to Jewish identity and Israeli nationalism. In the popular imagination of Jews everywhere, the oath that Israeli soldiers take, that Masada shall not fall again, also means that Israel must survive.

Theorizing Tourism: Analyzing Iconic Destinations by Arthur Asa Berger, 132–137.
© 2013 Left Coast Press, Inc. All rights reserved.

The Great Wall of China, one of the greatest wonders of the world, was listed as a World Heritage by UNESCO in 1987. Just like a gigantic dragon, the Great Wall winds up and down across deserts, grasslands, mountains and plateaus, stretching approximately 8,851.8 kilometers (5,500 miles) from east to west of China. With a history of more than 2,000 years, some of the sections are now in ruins or have disappeared. However, it is still one of the most appealing attractions all around the world owing to its architectural grandeur and historical significance.

Great Wall Facts:

Chinese Name: 长城/万里长城

Chinese Pinyin: Cháng Chéng/Wàn Lǐ Cháng Chéng. Length: 8,851.8 km (5,500 miles)

Construction Period: About 2,000 years from the Warring States Period (476 BC–221 BC) to Ming Dynasty (1368–1644)

www.travelchinaguide.com/china_great_wall/

The Great Wall of China is 1000 times longer than any [other] monument ever built in [the] history of mankind. Development of the Great Wall started before the birth of Christ & continued up to when Italian explorer Christopher Columbus sailed to America. Fear made the Chinese build the longest wall in the world, also known as the "longest cemetery ever built." This is because millions of poor Chinese peasants who worked to build the wall were buried in it when they died from exhaustion & pain. [The] Great Wall of China is where celebrities & the world's Presidents come to visit & pose. Also, millions of tourists visit every year. I looked up online to see exactly how many tourists visit the Great Wall each year and the number is 53,000 tourists a day starting from 2007. This number is quite low because the Chinese government imposed restrictions on how many people can visit the Wall each year due to wear & tear of the wall. Few tourists realize the Great Wall they are walking on & taking pictures of are [sic] younger than they are. This is because the Great Wall of China was recently renovated and rebuilt a few decades ago. The real Wall of China is rarely visited by tourists.

www.great-wall-of-china-facts.com/

Chapter 16

The Great Wall of China

There is a popular belief that The Great Wall of China has the distinction of being the only man-made work of architecture that is visible from outer space. It cannot be seen from outer space—at least as far as American astronauts are concerned, for that is what they have reported. The Great Wall of China is, however, the longest and most ambitious, large scale construction project in the history of mankind—a magnificent wall that stretches for 5,500 miles across China. That figure includes some natural areas that function as a defense against intruders. The wall was built to keep Mongols and other barbarians out and to help preserve Chinese culture. So it served two purposes: military defense and cultural reinforcement.

The Great Wall may be seen as a symbol reflecting China's continual search for security in a world with what it perceives as hostile forces all along its borders. Even today China has concerns about its security, which explains why in 2012 it is devoting a larger percentage of its budget for military weapons and the expansion of its army than in previous years. While China is, without a doubt, the most powerful country in Asia, it still harbors anxieties about neighboring countries such as India and Pakistan, both of which have atomic bombs.

The Great Wall is a UNESCO World Heritage Site. UNESCO describes its cultural and military significance as follows:

> The Great Wall of the Ming is, not only because of the ambitious character of the undertaking but also the perfection of its construction, a masterpiece. The wall constitutes, on the vast scale of a continent, a perfect example of architecture integrated into the landscape. During the Chunqiu period, the Chinese imposed their models of construction and organization of space in building the defence works along the northern frontier. The spread of Sinicism was accentuated by the population transfers necessitated by the Great Wall. (whc.unesco.org/en/list/438)

The UNESCO citation calls our attention to the fact that the wall is a beautiful structure and an enormous one, that it winds up and down hills for thousands of miles and that it is beautifully integrated into the environment. It's impossible for us to grasp the prodigious amount of work that was necessary to build this gigantic wall; we can only imagine how many millions of people worked on it over the many years of its construction, and how many workers died or were injured in building it. The human cost must have been staggering. If the people who died while building the wall are in fact buried in it, it is certainly the "world's longest graveyard."

The Great Wall, which took something like 2,000 years to construct, is also China's most popular tourist attraction, attracting close to 100 million foreign and domestic tourists a year. The section of the Great Wall near Beijing is the area that attracts most tourists. Tourists generally only see a small, heavily restored section of the wall. If you head 3,000 miles further west, you will see a wall that is made out of mud and is falling down. Ironically, then, the Great Wall, which was built to keep foreigners out, now serves to bring tourists into China—to marvel at the scope of the wall and its aesthetic qualities. As the quote in the epigraph points out, the sections of the Great Wall that most tourists visit have been reconstructed or renovated a number of decades ago, so they are not seeing the "real" Great Wall but a newly rebuilt part of it— a rebuilt wall, we must assume or hope that is very much like the original one. (In 2012 China opened several other restored parts of the Great Wall to tourists, in an effort to relieve some of the overcrowding and stress that the section of the Great Wall near Beijing is experiencing.)

When I visited the Great Wall, I could see it stretching for miles and miles from my vantage point. It is likely, of course, that the Chinese government built many miles of reconstructed wall near the places where tourists most often visit the Great Wall. The fact that the Great Wall has been renovated in popular tourist areas brings up the matter of authenticity in tourism studies. Do tourists want to see the "real" Great Wall, which may be in bad repair, or an inauthentic but more visually satisfying reconstruction of the Great Wall? The answer seems to be that authenticity is of little concern to contemporary postmodern tourists who want a satisfying experience rather than an authentic one that might not provide good photo opportunities. That point was made by Erik Cohen earlier in this book in his discussion of the impact of postmodern thought on tourism and the lack of concern in contemporary tourists for authenticity. For postmodern tourists, a restored Great Wall of China is more "Chinese" than a section of the Great Wall that is in disrepair and thus less interesting.

Walls are still part of the defensive strategy of many countries. In Israel, the government built a wall—a very controversial one as far as its placement was concerned —that separated Jewish areas from Arab areas. Once this wall was set up, the number of suicide bombings in Israel diminished greatly. So while the Israeli wall may not be as aesthetically pleasing as the Great Wall of China, the Israeli wall has been very functional and a great success, though it makes life more difficult for Palestinians, who have a hard time crossing into jobs in the Israeli sector, or visiting relatives. In the United States, the government is building a wall on the southern border to keep Mexican and other third world people from crossing the border illegally and entering and working in the United States. It is estimated that there are now 12 million illegal immigrants living in the United States, so it might be suggested that the wall is being built a few decades too late. There is also a question of how effective the wall will be when it is completed. It will be high-tech, but will it work?

The point is that walls are still used for defensive purposes and to keep outsiders out and insiders in. A subtext of the Great Wall of China might be that it also was designed to maintain the racial purity of the

Chinese people and prevent intermarriage and, literally, at the time, the "mongolization" of the Chinese people and Chinese culture. There is now another "Great Wall" in China and that is the "firewall" the Chinese authorities have erected around the internet in an attempt to prevent news and other information that the government doesn't want Chinese people to see from being accessed by the Chinese general public. As Deborah Fallows, a Senior Research Fellow with the Pew Internet and American Life project explains (2008):

> The Chinese government has long tried to control its internet in many ways. It censors or blocks politically-outspoken blogs. It has arrested citizens on charges of "inciting subversion" for posting articles in chat rooms critical of the Communist Party. It passes internet traffic through a "Great Firewall" designed to deny access to such international websites as Wikipedia, Technorati, all blogs hosted by Blogspot, and many sites maintained by the BBC. It also censors content on Chinese-based sites dealing with a host of topics, including the religious group Falun Gong, the 1989 Tiananmen incident, corruption among government officials, the independence movement in Taiwan, a free Tibet, various human rights issues, political incidents, or citizens' uprisings.

So, one way or another, the Great Wall exists in China; though now in a different "electronic" form, its function remains the same.

The Great Wall is an example of the power of rulers to create monuments of one kind or another—usually to glorify themselves but, as in the case of the wall, also to protect the Chinese people. These monuments are attractions for those international tourists who want to see, for themselves, the most important sites containing masterpieces of cultural significance and historic importance. Tourists don't think much about the thousands of peasants and slaves who work to build monuments like the pyramids in Egypt and the Great Wall. In the case of the Great Wall, in the epigraph we learned that the Great Wall has also been described as the longest graveyard in the world because of the huge numbers of peasants who died while working on it. History tends to focus attention on great rulers and leaders, who order monuments—forts, cathedrals, palaces, pyramids, Great Walls, and so on—to be built, and not on the common people, in many cases slaves, who actually do the work in building such monuments. It took millions of people to build the Great Wall, but they are lost to history, just as most people's lives do not attract the attention of historians. If it weren't for the desires of rulers of one kind or another, through the ages, to create monuments, often as a reflection of their narcissism, nationalism, and power, heritage tourists would have many fewer places to visit.

Theorizing Tourism: Analyzing Iconic Destinations by Arthur Asa Berger, 138–143.

The Great Pyramid of Giza stands on the northern edge of the Giza Plateau, located about 10 miles west of Cairo. It is composed of over 2 ½ million blocks of limestone, which weigh from 2 to 70 tons each. Its base covers over 13 acres and its volume is around 90,000,000 cubic feet. You could build 30 Empire State buildings with its masonry. It is 454 feet high which is equivalent to a modern 48-story building. There are currently 203 courses or steps to its summit. Each of the four triangular sides slope upward from the base at an angle of 51 degrees 51 minutes and each side has an area of 5 1/2 acres. The joints between adjacent blocks fit together with optical precision and less than a fiftieth of an inch separates the blocks. The cement that was used is extremely fine and strong and defies chemical analysis. Today, with all our modern science and engineering, we would not be able to build a Great Pyramid of Giza. The Great Pyramid is thought to have been erected around 2600 BC during the reign of Khufu (Cheops). Next to the Great Pyramid stand 2 additional large pyramids. The slightly smaller one is attributed to Cheop's son and successor, Kephren. The other, still smaller, is attributed to Kephren's successor, the grandson of Cheops, Mykerionos. To the south-east of the Great Pyramid lies the Sphinx. The total number of identified pyramids in Egypt is about 80.

www.gizapyramid.com/overview.htm

Chapter 17

The Great Pyramid at Giza, Egypt

Before the age of mass travel, relatively few people actually saw the remarkable pyramids in Egypt. Many people saw images of the pyramids in newspaper and magazine articles or in films or television programs, but relatively few people traveled to Egypt. With the development of air travel and mass tourism, now Egypt and the pyramids are quite accessible, and travel to Egypt is relatively reasonable. Around ten million tourists visited Egypt in 2011, a much smaller count than usual caused largely by the Egyptian revolution. Without the political unrest, Egypt is among the most visited tourist destinations in the world. Most tourists come to Egypt to see its monuments, which makes Egypt a site largely of cultural and heritage tourism. It is estimated that Egypt houses around a third of the world's most important cultural tourism sites. Though these include the Sphinx, Abu Simbel, the temples of Karnak, the Valley of the Kings, and the port of Alexandria, the most iconic site is the plateau of Giza adjacent to Cairo and its pyramids.

The Egyptians considered pyramids to be symbols of the Sun, the god Ra, and constructed them as the burial tombs of Egyptian kings in the Old and Middle Kingdoms (3100–1600 BC). Pharaohs were considered to be divine beings by the ancient Egyptians, so the pyramids had a religious significance of considerable importance. While we know the pyramids best from the three large ones at Giza, there are actually well over 100 pyramids identified along the Nile valley. It is estimated that it took between 20,000 and 30,000 workers to build the pyramids at Giza over a period of eighty years, and they were treated well by the Pharaoh. Each side of the Great Pyramid of Kheops, the largest, is 755 feet long. It is an astonishing feat of construction and is considered one of the seven wonders of the ancient world. It is, in fact, the only one of the seven wonders of the ancient world that is still standing.

In his book *The Great Pyramid: Ancient Egypt Revisited,* John Romer estimates that teams of twenty workers for each block would have been the most rational way to quarry the blocks. These teams, he suggested, would not have had great difficulty in moving the blocks from the quarry to the building site and pushing them up the ramps onto the structure. It would have taken around 12,000 quarry workers to mine the two million two-and-a-half-ton blocks over a dozen years. The standard size of the blocks minimized the difficulties of constructing the Great Pyramid. It is, for the most part, an example of what we now call "modular" construction. The bulk of archaeological information from excavations at Giza, hieroglyphic texts, scientific analysis, and religious and historical facts support this hypothesis.

The emotional power of these structures is such that there have been endless theories about how and when the pyramids were built. There is a curious book by Joseph Davidovits that argues that the Great Pyramid was not made of blocks cut from a quarry but was cast from a mixture of re-agglomerated stone that replicated the kind of stone found in a quarry and was used to build the Great Pyramid. Erik van Daniken proposed in his book *Chariots of the Gods* that they were the product of ancient spacemen visiting earth. Another theory holds that the blocks were lifted into place by kites. Mathematicians and pseudo-mathematicians have been working formulas for centuries, hoping to unlock some sort of pyramidal numerology.

What holds all of these theories together is the belief that ancient technology was insufficiently sophisticated to construct these buildings, the tallest human structures built before the twentieth century AD. This can be exemplified by David Jordan, who purports that "sonic levitation" was used to build the Great Pyramid:

> Let's face it, the many awesome stone structures of the ancients were not done by fulcrums, pulleys, slopes and manpower. It just wasn't possible!! And besides they could have never have placed them so precisely within fractions of an inch, as can be seen in their stonework. They have to have employed an unknown force, that we at present know little about ... and sonic stone levitation seems the most plausible. For even in the recent past, some people have seen the Tibetan Monks levitate huge stones by concentrating sound at the center of their semicircular trumpets and drums, so as to levitate them into place at a much higher elevation. (SEE http://www.crystalinks.com/levitationtibet.html.) And so considering this possibility, the same could have been done at Giza, as the whole Temple structure could have been built by sonic stone levitation, and even built as a levitation system for the souls of the Pharaoh, as it was much more than a mere tomb. Hence the following can make more sense to you in terms of frequencies (From members.aol.com/_ht a/ MetPhys/124quartzcheops.html). (www.davidjayjordan.com/SonicStone Levitation.html)

It is understandable that a building as remarkable as the Great Pyramid would attract all kinds of theories by those who feel that there arc mystical and secret aspects of the Great Pyramid that most people do not recognize or understand. Nonetheless, archaeologists have ample evidence of how they were built, even the names of the architects, without needing the aid of mystical forces or alien beings. The workers on the pyramids were not slaves but men and women who lived in villages devoted to housing the workers. And the workers felt that their work was important and helped contribute to the glory of Egypt. The *National Geographic* describes the role of the workers as follows:

> The builders were skilled, well-fed Egyptian workers who lived in a nearby temporary city. Archaeological digs on the fascinating site have

revealed a highly organized community, rich with resources, that must have been backed by strong central authority.

It's likely that communities across Egypt contributed workers, as well as food and other essentials, for what became in some ways a national project to display the wealth and control of the ancient pharaohs. Such revelations have led Zahi Hawass, secretary general of Egypt's Supreme Council of Antiquities and a National Geographic explorer-in-residence, to note that in one sense it was the Pyramids that built Egypt—rather than the other way around. (science.nationalgeographic.com/science/archaeology/giza-pyramids/)

We can think of the construction of the Great Pyramid as a gigantic public works project that helped create a unified Egypt. The comment, by Zahi Hawass— "It was the pyramids that built Egypt"—offers an important insight into the role of the government in modern states and the importance of government investments in public works, in the infrastructure and other projects that benefit the general public.

Modern societies follow this lead and build numerous projects, similar in size and scope to the Great Pyramid, to enhance the quality of life for their citizens and to provide work for them as well. In the United States, we built our great intercontinental highway system, countless bridges, and huge downtown skyscrapers. Majestic religious structures are also dominant buildings in our cities, mirroring the Egyptian desire to link monumental architecture with religious observance. And American equivalents to the Egyptian kings—our presidents—are also memorialized with impressive buildings such as the Washington Monument and Lincoln Memorial in Washington. Nor is this building of monuments limited to the United States, as many other countries have great structures devoted to deceased political and religious leaders, buildings that are often key tourist destinations.

Theorizing Tourism: Analyzing Iconic Destinations by Arthur Asa Berger, 144–149.

The Escorial is a vast building complex located in San Lorenzo de El Escorial, near Madrid, in central Spain. The building is the most important architectural monument of the Spanish Renaissance. Construction of El Escorial began in 1563 and ended in 1584. The project was conceived by King Philip II, who wanted a building to serve the multiple purposes of a burial place for his father, Holy Roman emperor Charles V; a Hieronymite monastery; and a palace. The first architect, Juan Bautista de Toledo, designed the ground plan on a gridiron scheme, recalling the grill on which San Lorenzo, the patron of the building, was martyred. After Toledo's death, Juan de Herrera took up work on the project. Although Herrera was influenced by the styles of Sebastiano Serlio and Giacomo Barozzi da Vignola, the final product was uniquely Spanish. The building complex, severe in its lines, has four principal stories with large towers at each corner. Arranged within a quadrangle, the buildings include: the church (1582); the monastery, royal palace, and college (1584); and the library (1592). The interior of the Escorial was decorated by many notable Spanish and Italian artists of the 16th and 17th centuries. Pellegrino Tibaldi and Federico Zuccaro were among the earliest painters to execute frescoes there. Other masters who painted works for the Escorial were El Greco, Luca Giordano, and Claudio Coello. An important collection of paintings by Renaissance and baroque artists donated by the crown is among the many artistic treasures housed in the complex.

www.el-escorial.com/

Chapter 18

El Escorial, Spain

El Escorial, with its 1600 paintings (some by great masters such as Goya, El Greco, and Velasquez) and 500 frescoes and its library and mortuary, had an impact on Spanish culture that was long lasting, and has a historical importance that might explain why it is such a popular tourist attraction. It attracts around 500,000 visitors a year. El Escorial is an easy day trip from Madrid, which has not just Spain's greatest museum but one of the world's greatest museums, the Prado.

A website that focuses upon the architectural significance of El Escorial offers this analysis of its significance:

> The ideology behind the design has also been the subject of debate. Traditionally it has been considered the embodiment of the most orthodox spirit of the Counter-Reformation and a reflection of the rigid mentality

of Philip and Herrera. The possible influence of hermetic thought and the mysticism of the philosopher Ramón Lull has been suggested, with the Escorial being conceived as a new Temple of Jerusalem, despite Sigüenza's rejection of formal links between the monastery's design and the Temple of Solomon. It has also been seen as relying on Early Christian principles, especially on such early models as the aesthetics of St. Augustine, as embodied in his City of God. Another suggestion, drawing on the writings of both Sigüenza and Herrera, is that it revived a Christian tradition of classical architecture, evident in its use of orders, its system of proportions and its 'cubism' or block-like design. (www. el-escorial.com/El-Escorial-Architecture.html)

This passage offers us an insight into the "philosophy" behind the design of the complex and suggests that this design is connected to religious thought and ties in to our notions of what the Temple of Solomon looked like and to classical Christian architecture.

The building, itself, as a work of architecture, can be seen as representing an attack on the Protestant reformation and a reaffirmation of Catholic theology and thought. Thus, Jose de Siguenza (1544–1606) explained that El Escorial was the architectural realization of a number of biblical prefigurations. El Escorial was like Noah's Ark in that it saved numerous souls who were fleeing from the deluge of the world, and it was like the Tabernacle of Moses in that it protected the ark in which God Himself dwelled, and from which He disseminated his numerous laws.

El Escorial can be seen as a manifestation or concretization of the Christian tradition of "typology" which interpreted events of the day as fulfillments of biblical events. In the Middle Ages, this theory affected architectural design and was meant to justify and consolidate Catholic religious thought. The architectural design of a complex like El Escorial can, then, be said to have a religious dimension to it—aside from the fact that the complex contained a church and a monastery. We may suggest that El Escorial's "geometrical severity" can be linked to the dogmas of the Spanish Catholic Church at the time and to Philip II's attempt to bolster the authority of the church and counter the impact of the Reformation.

What I remember most about my visit to El Escorial is that the place gave me the creeps. There is something I would describe as menacing about the façade of the building, and although it is beautiful inside and has a fabulous collection of art, I was very happy when my wife and I finished wandering around it and left. We spent more than three hours there.

18. *El Escorial, Spain*

It is a large complex that has many things in it; it is a seminary, a museum, a library with some 40,000 books, and a palace, and it has a mausoleum with the remains of all of the kings and queens of Spain after Charles V (with just a few exceptions). I had the uneasy feeling while wandering in El Escorial that, there, in the building, the Inquisition was still in full force and it would be only a matter of time before some guard would grab me and take me to an unwanted "interview" with a Grand Inquisitor.

This sense of dread that I had was rooted in the architecture of the complex and the preoccupation with death that I found in El Escorial. A British architect, Francis Haskell, discussed El Escorial in terms that tied the building to the *auto de fe* of the Spanish Inquisition. An auto de fé is the term describing the Spanish inquisition's process of judging and usually condemning a person to be burned at the stake for heresy. Haskell writes, "Why should the 'geometrical severity of the Escorial' have been 'the architectural corollary of the fierce *autos de fé* of Seville and Valladolid?'... Is there some general equation between geometrical severity and the treatment of heresy?" This passage is quoted in David Watkin's *Morality and Architecture Revisited* (2001:xvii). This notion that architecture can generate a certain mood in people is widely recognized. Think, for example, of the impact on our senses and feelings of being inside a gigantic cathedral like the one in Seville?

El Escorial raises the question of how tourists respond to architecture. In the case of El Escorial, the architectural severity of its design has, at the unconscious level, I would suggest, an impact on the psyches of the half million tourists who visit the site each year. There is also the preoccupation with death, with so many bodies of Spanish rulers in the building, that adds to a sense of unease that tourists may feel. Most tourists who visit El Escorial do so because it is considered an important building, for historical and religious reasons, and because it functions, among other things, as a museum with many treasures.

Theorizing Tourism: Analyzing Iconic Destinations by Arthur Asa Berger, 150–153.

When I began field work in Brasilia in 1980, one of my objectives was to link ethnographic activity with the set of critical attitudes known as modernism. By the latter I refer to the disenchantment of the avant-gardes— dadaism, surrealism, constructivism and futurism, among others, which arose in the context of European capitalism and which stood against it and bourgeois society. What drew me, as an anthropologist, was their subversive intent: differences not withstanding their aim was to disrupt the imagery of what bourgeois society understood as the real and the natural, to challenge the taken-for-granted, to defamiliarize, disorient, decode, deconstruct, and de-authenticate the normative, moral, aesthetic and familiar categories of social life.... My intention was to take modernism out of its usual domain in art and literature, and its generally internal readings in related fields of criticism, by showing how it becomes linked to social practices and thereby becomes a force in the social world.

James Holston, *The Modernist City: An Anthropological Critique of Brasilia*

Modern academies were formed at the major universities such as Cambridge and Harvard and from there the Purist doctrines of John Calvin Corbusier, Martin Luther Gropius, and John Knox vander Rohe were dispersed. Their white cathedrals, the black and white boxes of the International Style, were soon built in every land, and for a while the people and professors kept the faith. Ornament, polychromy, metaphor, humor, symbolism, and convention were put on the Index and all forms of decoration and historical reference were declared taboo. We are all acquainted with the results—"the architecture of good intentions"—as Colin Rowe termed them, and there are a lot of pleasant white housing estates and machine-aesthetic hospitals to prove that the intentions were not all misguided.

Charles Jencks, "Postmodern Vs. Late-Modern"

154

Chapter 19

Brasilia, Brazil

The quotation from James Holston's book on Brasilia raises an interesting question. What impact does modernist architecture have on our lives and, for our purposes, on the lives of the tourists who visit a modernist city? He offers Brasilia, the national capitol, as a quintessential example of architectural modernism in that it was planned by modernist urban designers and its buildings were designed by a modernist architect. And what has been described as a "utopian modernist" city was created according to their plans. Brasilia has also been described as a dystopian, anti-human modernist horror. Modernism in architecture replaced neo-classical, art nouveau, and Victorian styles of architecture, and was, in turn, replaced by postmodernist architecture and urban design.

Brasilia has the honor of being the largest "planned" city we have. It only took around five years to build and was plunked down in the center of a desert area in Brazil, in 1960, with the notion that it would be more accessible to Brazilians in all parts of a very large country. It has many

modernist buildings—that means it is full of concrete slab construc-
tions with a great deal of steel and glass and with little ornamentation.
Some critics have said Brasilia was designed for automobiles, not tourists,
because there are few places to congregate and walking in Brasilia is not
facilitated. As the supreme example of a city created by design, it is of
particular interest to tourists interested in modern architecture and urban
design. *The Lonely Planet* describes Brasilia as follows:

> Brazil's futuristic capital is the closest attempt on earth to a create a
> modern utopia. It's the result of a long-harnessed Brazilian dream of an
> inland capital, carved out of nowhere in the 1950s in a spectacular feat of
> urban planning, architectural design and political prophecy.
>
> The purpose-built city and its surrounding area, known as the
> Distrito Federal (DF), occupies part of the Brazilian central plateau—
> the Planalto—totaling 5802 sq km, with rolling hills and a large artificial
> lake, Paranoá. Wide-open, spectacular cerulean skies characterize the
> whole area, a picturesque backdrop to Brasília's clean-lined design and
> marvelous architecture.
>
> For a nation often tapped as the country of the future, Brasília is
> its revolutionary testament to that end, a living museum lauded the
> world over for everything from its avant-garde grid of perfectly planned
> streets to its über-organized residential apartment and commercial
> blocks. As Brazil's seat of government, it's a city of bureaucrats and
> government workers, all of whom relish the national capital as a '60s
> version of a third-millennium city. It remains the only city in the world
> constructed in the 20th century to achieve World Cultural Heritage
> designation by Unesco. (www.lonelyplanet.com/brazil/the-central-west/
> brasilia#ixzz1wYPeuaif)

This description deals with the utopian aspirations of those who created Brasilia. Whether it is a modernist utopia or dystopia, as I suggested
above, is open to question. It is yet another UNESCO World Heritage
Site, and thus it is of interest to tourists who want to visit great buildings
and unusual cities. Many tourists visit ancient sites to find out what life in
the distant past was like. Tourists who visit Brasilia get an idea of what life
in the future may be like.

Modernism

Virginia Woolf described the moment in December 1910 when the Victorian period ended and modernism suddenly became dominant. She wrote:

> On or about December, 1910, human character changed. I am not saying that one went out, as one might into a garden, and there saw a rose had flowered, or that a hen had laid an egg. The change was not like that. But a change there was, nevertheless, and since one must be arbitrary, let us date it about the year 1910....When human relations change, there is at the same time a change in religion, conduct, politics, and literature.

This material is from her lecture "Mr. Bennett and Mrs. Brown" that she gave at a meeting of the Heretics Club at Cambridge University in 1924. She argued that after December 1910 (or around then) life in England had changed in major ways—a change that she noticed in the relationships between husbands and wives, masters and servants, children and parents, and the kind of literature that was being written. Scholars have described this change as the advent of modernism, which is reflected in the work of writers such as of James Joyce, Ezra Pound, and Robert Musil and the dominance of modernist architectural styles.

Let me say something about modernism in architecture and culture and contrast it with the movement that replaced it, postmodernism. I have already dealt with postmodernism in architecture in my chapters on Las Vegas and Frank Gehry's Guggenheim Museum in Bilbao. In rough terms, we can say that Modernism became a cultural dominant from approximately 1900 to 1960, when it lost favor and was replaced by Postmodernism.

Modernist architecture is characterized by the following:

Avoiding ornamentation

Great use of steel, glass, and concrete

Focus on functionalism ("form follows function")

Simplicity of form

Rejection of previous styles

Rational use of materials

It is difficult to define architectural modernism because there were several movements that can be classified as modernist, such as the "International Style."

There is an interesting irony about modernism in architecture that is pointed out by Jack Solomon in his book *Signs of Our Times: The Secret Meanings of Everyday Life*. He writes (1990:118):

> Gropius meant to "start from zero," to begin all over with a rationally efficient, geometrically pure architectural style suited to a century of industrial democracy. Envisioning a socialist future, the architects of the Bauhaus School set about creating a proletarian architecture purged of the ornamental detailing of feudal and bourgeois architectural design. No more vaulted ceilings, pitched roofs, masonry fronts, cornices, pillars, fancy colors, colonnades, or gables. The future was to be written in concrete, glass, and steel, painted white or gray, and shaped in pure, boxlike forms (recall Pruitt-Igoe). The interiors of the new buildings were to be ascetically bare: no moldings, wainscoting, mantelpieces, or cornices; just clean, unadorned lines and white walls. In short, the industrial age was to get an industrial architecture. Everything from the new workers' housing projects to office buildings and private homes would have the severely functional lines of a factory or boiler room.
>
> But a funny thing happened on the way to the future. Rather than sweeping aside the forces of bourgeois capitalism, the Modern designs of the Bauhaus School became the favored patterns of capitalist contractors, who began to fill the cities of the world with Modernist office towers, housing projects, and hotel complexes with the same boxy structures built of glass and steel and concrete.

Among the most important modernist architects were Walter Gropius, who founded the Bauhaus School in Germany, the Swiss architect Le Corbusier, and the Dutch architect Mies van der Rohe. They influenced many architects in many other countries.

Most middle-aged contemporary postmodern architects were trained by modernist architects, since modernism dominated our architectural thought until the sixties or seventies. Frank Gehry would be an example of a postmodernist architect (or, perhaps, post-postmodernist) who had been trained by modernist architecture professors, though Gehry doesn't like to describe himself as postmodernist. If there was a moment when modernist architecture can be said to have imploded, it was when the modernist Pruitt-Igoe's housing development in Saint Louis was destroyed by dynamite on July 15, 1972, because it was so dysfunctional. . The complex was designed by a celebrated modernist architect, Minoru Yamasaki, who also designed The World Trade Center Towers.

This discussion of architectural Modernism is relevant because Brasilia must be described as an exemplary Modernist city—and was designed as such from scratch. Brasilia is based upon the work of the urban planner Lucio Costa and the architect Oscar Niemeyer. They started working on it in 1956, and Brasilia was built in just a few years, formally opening on April 22, 1960, as the national capital of Brazil. Le Corbusier was instrumental in choosing the team that designed the city and its buildings. Brasilia is interesting because it offers us an example of the impact of modernist thought and design on people's lives.

In a review by Peter Hall of *The Modernist City: An Anthropological Critique of Brasilia* by James Holston (1990), we learn about the impact of modernist theory on architecture and urban design. Holston discusses the architectural movement led by Le Corbusier and Gropius that culminated in the Congres Internationaux d'Architecture Modern (the CIAM) in the 1930s, which had a radical intent—to replace capitalism with a new social order that was collectivist in nature. He suggests that the godfather of Brasilia was the leading Brazilian architect Oscar Niemeyer, who was a Communist. Niemeyer persuaded a competition jury that was set up to approve a design for Brasilia to accept the one made by Lucio Costa, his teacher. Peter Hall describes what happened:

> This plan, according to Holston, was the ultimate political achievement of the modern movement, "a CIAM city . . . the most complete example ever constructed of the architectural and planning tenets put forward in CIAM manifestoes"; it achieved the objective for which the pioneers of the modern movement had struggled in vain. Its hidden agenda was to create a totally new-built form as a shell for a new society, without reference to history: The past was simply to be abolished. "Brasilia," he writes, "was built to be more than the symbol of this new age. Rather, its design and construction were intended as a means to *create* it by transforming Brazilian society."
>
> Brasilia thus embodied a fundamental premise of the modern movement: "total decontextualization," in which a utopian future becomes the means to measure the present, without any sense of historical context. Costa introduces his plan, in disarmingly self-effacing fashion, as the carrier of a mythic idea that came to him almost as a vision: It provides a basis for a city created on a clean slate, without reference to the past.

Thus, a Utopian city, Brasilia, was built according to Modernist precepts, and what you got, for some critics, was an inhuman horror. Robert

Hughes, an art critic, described Brasilia as "a utopian horror.…It is a ceremonial slum infested with Volkswagens." The Russian astronaut Yuri Gargarin said, "The impression I have is that I'm arriving on a different planet." And Julian Dibbel described Brasilia as "intended, after all, to give the impression of having been built neither by nor for mere earthlings. A race of hyperintelligent Volkswagens, perhaps, or aliens who speak a language made up entirely of Euclidean axioms, might be expected to feel at home in this sidewalk-poor zone of perfectly circulating asphalt arteries and relentlessly clean lines of design—but not any species as puny and unkempt as homo sapiens."

But over the years a process called "Brazilianization" has taken place, with stores springing up and trees growing to maturity, and Brasilia is now a much more humane city, defenders of Brasilia argue. And just as Brasilia has been Brazilianized, so has Brazil undergone a process we might describe as Brasilianation, with Brasilia's impact growing stronger in Brazilian architecture. Brasilia plays a role as a symbol of Brazil's economic power and aesthetic daring. But Brasilia's problems suggest that it isn't easy to plan anything as big and complicated as a city. Many modernist buildings are beautiful and functional, and modernism has played an important role in architecture, but as the Pruitt-Igoe disaster suggests, modernism doesn't work for everyone, and an entire city of modernist buildings may be too much of a good thing.

Brazil gets more than five million tourists in a typical year, but most of the tourists who visit Brasilia go there because they are interested in modernist architecture and urban design. The UNESCO World Heritage description of Brasilia explains its importance to cultural tourists as follows:

> Brasilia, a capital created ex nihilo in the centre of the country in 1956, was a landmark in the history of town planning. The 20th-century principles of urbanism, as expressed by Le Corbusier, have rarely been applied on the scale of capital cities. Only two noteworthy exceptions exist: Chandigarh and Brasilia. Its creators intended that every element, from the layout of the residential and administrative districts (often compared to the shape of a bird in flight) to the symmetry of the buildings themselves, should be in harmony with the city's overall design. The official buildings, in particular, are innovative and imaginative. (whc. unesco.org/en/list/445)

Brasilia is one of only two modern cities created to reflect Le Corbusier's modernist approach to architecture, and thus it is of considerable cultural importance. Just as tourists visit Bilbao to see Frank Gehry's Guggenheim Museum, so do tourists, generally with specialized interests, visit Brasilia to see one of only two cities that were created "out of nothing" and are considered exemplars of modernist architecture and urban design.

For tourists interested in visiting unusual cities and for those curious about what a "utopian" city is like, Brasilia is a unique destination. The same kind of tourists who go to Bilbao to see Frank Gehry's Guggenheim museum would be attracted to Brasilia, to see what a modernist "utopian" city is actually like. It also helps that Brazil has many other cities not very distant from Brasilia that are of interest to tourists.

Theorizing Tourism: Analyzing Iconic Destinations by Arthur Asa Berger, 154–161.

Siem Reap has managed to transform itself into one of Cambodia's fastest growing city and into a major tourist hub. In fact, tourism has become one of the most important industries contributing to the overall economic recovery and development of Cambodia. Tourism is one of the largest contributors to the Cambodian economy after the agriculture and textile industry and is the second largest income generator after the garment industry. For example, tourism generated tourism receipts of US$1.56 billion in 2009 with more than 2 million visitors.

Today, Siem Reap has emerged as a vibrant and exciting city with hotels and modern amenities, and it has pretty much continued to conserve much of its distinctive image, culture, traditions and architecture. In fact, besides its economic advantages, the Cambodian government views tourism as an effective tool to promote the cultural values and identity of Cambodia which had been lost given the excessive external interventions. An example of which is the Angkor temples. While the Angkor temples have always existed, the Khmers have always regarded it as a religious site and never thought of it as a symbol of national pride. Today, Angkor has become the symbol of nationalism and Cambodian identity, with a recent UNESCO/Trip Advisor survey declaring the Angkor as the most recommended World Heritage site.

blogs.cornell.edu/siemreapmasterclass/2011/02/27/
history-of-siem-reaps-tourism/

Fourteen years ago, there was but a single hotel (the faded Grand) in Siem Reap, then a sleepy village near the temples. Now, there are over 100, some charging $1,000 a night, plus a pub street bubbling with activity, exquisite art galleries and a growing collection of spas, along with legions of massage parlors and brothels. "Siem Reap is buzzing," enthuses Tourism Minister Lay Prohas, who compares its art and restaurant scene to Bali, only at much better prices. "New restaurants, hotels and pubs are opening every day. It has become stylish, classy." Critics say little benefit has reached locals. Squatter camps line the river; Siem Reap remains one of Cambodia's poorest provinces. Local businessmen say corruption is rampant, with bribery taking the place of permitting and planning.

www.gluckman.com/AngkorTourism.html

Chapter 20

Angkor Wat, Cambodia

Angkor Wat is the most important tourist site in Cambodia and the reason that Siem Reap, which is where most tourists visiting Angkor Wat stay, is full of huge hotels. As you drive on the road from the airport to the center of the city, you see row after row of large hotels, on either side of the road. Siem Reap is booming, though researchers into the impact of tourism in Siem Reap point out that most of the inhabitants there are not benefitting from the increase in tourism and are, actually, suffering, since prices of things have increased and most of the tourism dollars are not employed to better their lives. It is, like many of the tourist sites discussed in this book, a UNESCO World Heritage site.

Because of Angkor Wat's size, it is very difficult for visitors to get a sense of its totality. Even when the weather is not oppressively hot, it is so tiring walking around the many monuments in Angkor Wat in the morning that most tours give tourists a long lunch break to rest and recuperate from their morning's viewing.

The site is run by a private company, and there is a good deal of controversy about what happens to the money it collects from the tourists and whether it should be operated by the Cambodian government for the benefit of the Cambodian people. It costs foreign tourists $40 a person for a one day visit to Angkor Wat, and to that one can add the cost of a guide and of transportation. My point is that it is expensive for foreign tourists to visit Angkor Wat.

The explosion of tourism to Angkor Wat has not helped the local people, as the Gluckman quote at the beginning of this chapter suggests. One of the problems created by tourism, especially the kind of mass tourism found in Angkor Wat, is that because of corruption and political arrangements, often local people do not benefit from the money spent by tourists. Thus, we have the same situation that exists in Chichen Itza and many other sites where indigenous people live in the areas where the tourist attractions are found. These indigenous people do not benefit as much as they should from the money spent by tourists. They may, in fact, be penalized, because the cost of living in these areas often rises considerably as the tourist attractions become more popular.

A visit to Angkor Wat involves seeing many temples, spread out over a number of miles, which explains why it takes so long to see the most important parts of the temple complex. Many tourists purchase three day tickets, because there is so much to see in Angkor Wat. There is the Bayon Temple and, a tourist favorite, the Ta Prohm Temple, with huge trees and vines covering many of the buildings. There are also many other temples and sites of interest.

A guidebook that we purchased during our visit to Angkor Wat, *Along the Royal Road to Angkor* by Yoshiaki Ishizawa, provides an interesting insight into the religious importance of the site (2008:9):

> Angkor Wat, built in the early part of the twelfth century by the Angkor ruler Suryavarman II, is a Hindu temple. It was constructed as a royal tomb, and its central sanctuary housed an image of Shiva. Three concentric galleries enclose the central sanctuary, rising as one approaches the center of the complex....There are towers at each of the four corners of the innermost gallery, and the taller central sanctuary rises in their center, the peak of Mount Meru, the very center of the world. It was here, in this sacred space, that the secret ceremony uniting

the king and the god was conducted. Carvings of *devitas,* female deities, appear throughout the temple, and the galleries display scenes from the ancient Indian epic the *Mahabharata,* as well as other Hindu myths, heightening the drama of this holy citadel.

A later Kmer king, Jayavarman VII, became a follower of Buddhism, and he built the Bayon Temple as a symbol of Mount Sumenu, which for Buddhista was considered to be the center of the world. When visiting Angkor Wat, you often see orange robed Buddhist monks there, since it is now an important religious site for Buddhists.

This notion that Angkor Wat is in the "center of the world" is one of the fundamental aspects of religious thought. In his book *The Sacred and the Profane,* Mircea Eliade, a scholar of religion, explains that there is a difference between the way religious and non-religious people relate to space. For religious people, space is not homogenous, more or less all the same. Religious people see some spaces as qualitatively different—spaces that we can define as "sacred" as contrasted with profane space, which is all the same. Sacred spaces provide religious man and woman with a fixed point that guides his or her orientation to the world—just the opposite of the view of profane man and woman that all space is the same.

As Eliade explains (1961:22):

So it is clear to what a degree of discovery- –that is, the revelation—of a sacred space possesses existential value for religious man; for nothing can begin, nothing can be *done,* without a previous orientation—and any orientation implies acquiring a fixed point. It is for this reason that religious man has always sought to fix his abode at the "center of the world.".…

Revelation of a sacred space makes it possible to obtain a fixed point and hence to acquire orientation in chaos of homogeneity, to "found the world" and to live in a real sense.

From this perspective, Angkor Wat was, as Yoshiaki Ishizawa points out in his guidebook, at the "center of the world" for Suryavarman II and the pivot point from which his kingdom expanded. The reason sacred spaces need fixed points is that they enable religious people to make distinctions between sacred and profane space, have a reference point to evaluate things, and, ultimately, see the world differently from profane man and woman.

Angkor Wat, like all holy temples, can be seen, from a religious perspective, as both an image of the world—semiotically speaking, a *synecdoche* or a part that stands for the whole—and also a means of resanctifying the world. A visit to the temple, then, helps with the sanctification of the world. Although most tourists who visit Angkor Wat are not aware of the sacred significance of what they are doing, from the perspective of religious thought, visiting a sacred space like Angkor Wat is also a means of helping to sanctify the world. The symbolic significance of the Ankor Wat temples is lost on most visitors, to whom these sites are more like museum exhibits than living and real holy places with sacred significance. Tourists may know that the temples are "sacred," but that means relatively little to them, and they do not recognize that the monks in colorful outfits they see walking through the courtyards of the temples of Angkor Wat are partaking of a ritual that honors the temples as a center of the world or that has some other religious purpose.

The fact that visiting Angkor Wat is, for most people, something of an ordeal would only add to the notion that visiting the site has an unconscious religious dimension to it. It is generally very hot in Siem Reap, there are huge mobs of people visiting the monument at certain times, and walking in the ruins requires constant attention since it is easy to stumble. This would mean that a visit to Angkor Wat is, from the religious perspective, the culmination of a pilgrimage that tourists make—not that different from pilgrimages that religious people make to holy places, except that visitors to Angkor Wat do not consciously see their sightseeing there as religious in nature. All visits to religious sites, such as cathedrals, mosques, and temples of all kinds, have, from Eliade's perspective, a "sacred" dimension to them.

16% of American workers say they are too busy to take off all the vacation days that are due to them.

20% of American workers never take vacations.

13 days of vacation is the average in the United States and 42 days in Europe.

33% of American workers check in with their bosses during vacations.

40% of American workers skip summer vacations because of increased workloads and tighter budgets.

Statistics from various internet sources

Travel is a common, frequent, everyday occurrence in our present. In fact, it is a source of our commonality, as in 1987 over forty million Americans traveled abroad, and many more at home. Comprising less than 5 percent of the world's population, U.S. citizens accounted for over 25 percent of the world's spending for domestic and international travel—estimated at $2.3 trillion. If one counts all the California trips and journeys seasonally made, north and south, it is not merely a metaphor to say America is on the move and connected through mobilities. Travel, in the form of tourism, has become increasingly pervasive in our world. By the turn of the millennium, it will be the most important sector of world trade, surpassing oil, and is currently the second largest retail industry in the United States. The impression of the commonality of travel is intensified when one includes in the ranks of travelers those who obviously belong but do not appear in tourism statistics—business travelers, nomads, commuters, itinerant laborers, refugees, members of the armed services, diplomatic personnel, temporary and permanent immigrants.

Eric J. Leed, *The Mind of the Traveler: From Gilgamesh to Global Tourism.*

Chapter 21

Coda

Tourists have many needs. They have to get from where they live to where they want to go, which may involve a bus or a taxi to an airport, a wait in that airport for an hour or two, a flight on an airplane, a taxi to a hotel, booking a room in a hotel, dining in a restaurant, transportation to a desired site, hiring a guide, paying for admission to the site, hiring a cab or taking a bus back to a hotel, finding restaurants to eat lunch and dinner, and so on.

A Typical First Day of a Trip

Let us suppose an independent traveler and his wife, the Smiths, fly to India to see the Taj Mahal and, later, other places of interest to tourists. After they settle into their hotel, they may go out for a walk, and while they are walking, they may do a bit of shopping. Research shows that aside from visiting sites of interest, shopping for gifts and souvenirs is one of the most important parts of tourism Wherever you have tourist attractions, you generally have many opportunities to purchase things, and that is because tourists, generally speaking, want to buy all kinds of things and have money to spend on these things. Then they go to visit the Taj Mahal and attend an Indian dance show in the evening. They will leave Agra next morning for another destination. We can see the complications involved in travel and tourism that the Smiths experience in the chart below:

Before the Trip

buying guide books for the country: Lonely Planet, Rough Guides, etc.
using the internet to book flights and hotels
using the internet to look at travel blogs, TripAdvisor, etc.

The First Day of the Trip

getting to airport	taxi drivers or bus drivers **tip 1**
flight on plane	clerks, pilots, flight attendants
entering country	government agents. Visa payments
waiting for luggage	airport employees
getting to hotel	taxi drivers, bus drivers **tip 2**
registering in hotel	desk clerks

going to room	hotel staff **tip 3**
shopping	payments for purchases
getting to Taj Mahal	taxi drivers or bus drivers **tip 4**
buying tickets for site	clerks at site
seeing site	guides. payment and **tip 5**
having lunch	waiters, cooks, dishwashers. Pay for meal **tip 6**
returning to hotel	cab drivers, bus drivers **tip 7**
going to room	clerks
having dinner	waiters, cooks, etc. Payment for dinner **tip 8**
going to dance show	cab drivers, bus drivers **tip 9**
paying for tickets	clerks at theaters
seeing show	dancers, musicians, etc.
returning to hotel	cab drivers, bus drivers **tip 10**
getting key	clerks
sleep	
pack to leave hotel	money for chamber maids **tip 11**

END OF DAY ONE.

There are quite a few steps that have to be taken, payments to be made, and tips for services that are involved in this trip's first day. The Smiths would be tipping someone, for some service, eleven times during this first day and interacting with quite a number of people. In very poor countries, tips play an important role in the lives of those with whom tourists interact, so there are positive aspects to tipping. A dollar (or whatever) means little to an American tourist and may mean a great deal to an Indian worker.

Tourists who book group tours don't have to continually be spending money because they pay up front, and most of the details and payments are taken care of by the travel company. Spending money at so many steps and tipping so often is irritating, which explains why many tourists book group tours with travel companies that are more or less all-inclusive. Most people who visit India, and this applies to many other countries, book tours with tourism companies and are what Cohen described as either organized mass tourists or individual mass tourists. There are, of course, some explorers and drifters who do India (and other countries as well) on their own, but they are relatively rare. If the Smiths booked a hotel near the Taj Mahal and near the dance theater, they would save money on cab fares, but they would still be spending money continually and paying tips frequently.

We can imagine the Smiths in the center of a circle, and revolving around them are all the people with whom they interact on the first day of their trip. One reason the tourism industry is so large is that there are so many different companies involved in tourism: companies that build airplanes, companies that sell fuel to airline companies, automobile and bus manufacturers, cab fleets, cab drivers, bus companies and bus drivers, hotels, restaurants, theater companies, book publishers (of tourist guides), and many other kinds of companies and organizations. In short, there are a vast number of companies involved in the Smiths' travel, and they all can be considered as part of the tourism industry.

But what motivated the Smiths to decide to go to see the Taj Mahal rather than go to see Angkor Wat is a subject of increasing interest to tourism scholars. And why did they decide to visit India as free independent travelers (FITS) rather than book a tour with one of the many Indian travel agencies? Were they influenced by an "Incredible India" advertisement or commercial they saw? What impact did their using the internet to get information about India have? Did a friend who had been to India rave about it? Do they like Indian food? And how did they deal with anxieties that many travelers have about getting sick in India? What made them choose to stay at one hotel rather than another?

In the case of the Taj Mahal, we might assume that the Smiths had heard about how beautiful the building is and used a visit to see the Taj Mahal as one reason to visit India. They may think of India as "exotic" and be attracted by that aspect of a visit to India. India is also relatively inexpensive—or it can be, that is, if one doesn't insist on staying at five star hotels—and that also may have been a factor in their decision making.

All of the iconic buildings and places I discussed in this book attract tourists because they are seen as "world class" attractions, and many of them are UNESCO sites. And just as tourists are motivated to see famous places and buildings, I was guided by the notion that my book should discuss these places and buildings as a means of dealing with tourism as a subject for analysis and study. I have explained that there are a variety of gratifications that different kinds of tourism offer, such as seeing beautiful buildings, finding an outlet for sexual desires, and developing an identity as a "world traveler." Medical tourism is not an important part of travel and that may play a role in someone's decision to visit India, or any other country that offers these services. I have used these icons to suggest topics and themes that are connected with them, so this book is both descriptive and analytical, and my discussions of these icons use semiotic theory (the term "icon" is from semiotics) and related theories to unpack their cultural significance. In some sites, such as Chichen Itza, there are continual battles between indigenous people who wish to sell goods and the people who control the sites. In some famous sites, the money from tourists who visit the sites has not improved the lives of the people who live near them. That, unfortunately, is also the case with Angkor Wat.

Many of the sites I deal with in the book have a religious significance. Masada is where hundreds of Jews committed suicide rather than become slaves to the Romans. It has both a religious (for Jews) and nationalistic (for Israelis) significance. The Potala Palace is the seat of Tibetan Buddhism and the center of an international battle between China and the Tibetan people and their leader, during their Diaspora, the Dalai Lama. St. Basil's cathedral is a Russian Orthodox building that provides, I suggest, a bit of comic relief to the heaviness of Red Square and serves as a reminder of the marvelous Russian sense of humor that is reflected in the great comic Russian novels by Gogol and Bulgakov. Angkor Wat is the remains of an enormous ancient temple complex. El Escorial is a combination of museum and religious complex, with a monastery and a church in its confines. The rock garden at Ryoan-ji Temple in Kyoto also is a religious building, one of Kyoto's many remarkable temples. The Great Pyramid also has a religious significance and was built to house the body of the Pharaoh.

Because there are so many different kinds of tourists and because tourists all have different interests, incomes, levels of education, and passions, we may say that they all find different things in the tourist sites they visit that are meaningful to them. A visit to a religious site by a pilgrim has a much different meaning to that pilgrim than it does to someone who is motivated not by religious passion but by curiosity, and perhaps a passion for taking photographs.

Las Vegas and Disneyland represent two of America's most popular contributions to iconic places. As I show in various chapters, Disneyland has exerted a considerable influence on the development of consumer cultures.. French scholars like Baudrillard have been fascinated (maybe obsessed) by Disneyland and all that it represents.

I've dealt with two cities—Brasilia and Luang Prabang—that are both shaped by governmental planners and that are polar opposites in terms of their aesthetics. Brasilia is an example of urban city planning and modernist architecture. For some critics, Brasilia is a monstrosity, an inhuman city where there's no place to walk. Others see it as developing a tolerable lifestyle as it becomes "Brazilianized." Luang Prabang is a city where walking around is facilitated and where tourists find ways to relax and enjoy the wonderful restaurants and coffee shops, the night market, and the quality of life.

21. *Coda*

There are two relatively recent buildings in my analysis of icons—the Eiffel Tower and the Frank Gehry designed Guggenheim Museum in Bilbao. The Eiffel Tower is the subject of a remarkable essay by the French Marxist-semiotician Roland Barthes. I quoted part of this essay at the beginning of the chapter on the Eiffel Tower. It was considered a monstrosity by many people when it was built, but now it is considered to be beautiful and functions as a signifier of Paris, in particular, and France, in general. The Guggenheim Museum is generally considered to be the most important building of its time, one that released architects from the box form of modernism but isn't, according to Gehry, a postmodernist building. Some architectural critics suggest it isn't a building at all. It has played an important role in putting Bilbao, where it is located, on the tourist map.

Antarctica is a frozen desert, whose beauty attracts tourists, but the number of tourists who can land on Antarctica is limited, because the environment is quite fragile. It can be cited as an example of the success of sustainable tourism in helping to preserve an important tourist site by controlling the number of people who are allowed to land on it. There are a number of ocean lines that sail by Antarctica but don't land on it, providing tourists with marvelous photo-opportunities, which is all that matters for some tourists. Bali can be seen as the opposite of Antarctica—a tropical paradise full of flowers. Its inhabitants are Hindus, and they have created an extremely interesting culture in which religion permeates every aspect of their lives.

Finally, we have the Great Wall of China, the most massive structure ever built, stretching more than 5,000 miles in length, and the most important tourist attraction in China. It was built to keep Mongols and other peoples out and to help maintain Chinese culture. I suggest that the "wall" that the Communist government keeps around the internet can be seen as an analogue of the Great Wall—one that is meant to have the same function. One of the ironies connected with the Great Wall is that it was meant to keep foreigners out and now functions to attract foreign tourists.

We can say, about the iconic buildings and places I analyzed, that there's a great deal more than meets the eye in all of them, and that a knowledge of mythology, history, and politics, along with an understanding of semiotics and cultural theory, helps us more completely understand these icons and their significance for the tourists who visit them and their role in the societies in which they are found.

Theorizing Tourism: Analyzing Iconic Destinations by Arthur Asa Berger, 168–173.

Applications and Exercises

The questions and assignments that follow are meant to help you to apply what you have learned and, in some cases, to do research on aspects of tourism dealt with in this book. Please justify all your answers, explaining what facts you have gathered or what theories you are using to come to the conclusions you reach. Your instructor may have modifications of these questions or other questions for you to consider.

1.

You've read about the "national style of touring" of Japanese visitors to Bali. Using resources on the internet and in the library (in books and tourism journals) investigate the "national styles" of touring of people from:

United States	Germany
France	England
China	Italy

2.

Based on the discussions in the book of the various types of tourists in the first chapter, what kinds of tourists would be attracted to the following sites, and why:

Antarctica	The Masada
The Taj Mahal	Brasilia
Disneyland	Potala Palace

3.

What unrecognized myths might motivate tourists to visit:

Las Vegas	Bali
Disneyland	Tibet
Chichen-Itza	El Escorial

4.

How important is "authenticity" in attracting tourists? Investigate this topic in scholarly books and tourism journals and see what conclusions you come to.

5.

Investigate research on the connection between the age of tourists and the place they occupy on the Plog continuum? Do tourism scholars find weaknesses in his typology? Do you agree with Plog or with his critics?

6.

What relationship exists between demographics and the various kinds of tourism? How do factors like age, socio-economic class, ethnicity, race, and religion affect decision making by tourists.

7.

How do you define the term "exotic"? Is Hawaii an "exotic" destination? Explain your answer. Do some research, and based on it, make a list of the most "exotic" tourist destinations in terms of their degree of exoticism. Compare your list with those of others in the class.

8.

Dean MacCannell writes in his book *The Tourist* that the tourist is "one of the best models available for modern-man-in-general." Given our discussion of modernism, why do you think he made that statement?

9.

If you had unlimited funds, which of the iconic spots discussed in this book would you visit first? Why? Make a list of the top five icons discussed in the book in order of their interest to you and compare your list with those made by others in your class. What do you learn from this exercise?

10.

What is so remarkable about the Frank Gehry Guggenheim Museum in Bilbao, which is supposed to have "put Bilbao on the map?" Investigate the impact of the museum by comparing statistics on tourism in Bilbao before and after it was built. Do some research in scholarly books and articles about the Guggenheim museum's impact on tourism and on assessments of the museum as an important building.

11.

If you wanted to put some large city in the United States "on the tourist map," how would you do it? Explain how your efforts would attract tourists.

12.

What gratifications do tourists obtain from visiting the following places (or any other site assigned to you by your professor):

Las Vegas	The Great Pyramid in Egypt
Tibet	Chichen-Itza
The Great Wall of China	Disneyland

13.

How much can you trust of what you read on the internet about important tourist destinations. Compare your firsthand knowledge of a destination you've visited with what you read about it on the internet.

14.

Read an issue of *The Annals of Tourism Research,* the most important scholarly tourism journal. Make a list of the theories used by the authors and the concepts that they used. What insights does this list give you into the nature of tourism and the kinds of questions tourism scholars investigate.

15.

What are the five most interesting insights or ideas or concepts that you gained from reading this book? Has it made you look at tourism in a different light? Has it changed the way you view travel? Compare your top five insights to those of others in your class.

16.

Compare the way different travel guide books write about one of the sites dealt with in this book. Are there important differences? Do they generally reach the same conclusions? What did this exercise teach you about guide books?

17.

What areas of sacred space exist in your city? In your state? In the United States? Explain your answers. Investigate what tourism scholars have written about space and tourism.

18.

Investigate scholarly articles on tipping. What does research on this topic suggest about various aspects of tipping relative to national styles of tourism and other matters?

19.

Apply Freud's Id/Ego/Superego theory to aspects of tourism. Does Freud's theory enable you to see things in a different way?

20.

A publisher asks you to write a book on tourism. What book would you write? Describe it in a paragraph. Why would you write that particular book?

Theorizing Tourism: Analyzing Iconic Destinations by Arthur Asa Berger, 174–177.

References

Abram, Simone, Jacqueline Waldren, and Donald V. I. McLeod, Eds. 1997.
Tourists and Tourism: Identifying With People and Places.
Oxford, England: Berg.

Adler, Elkan Nathan. 1930.
Jewish Travelers.
London: Routledge.

Bailey, Martin.
www.forbes.com/2002/02/20/0220conn.html

Bakhtin, M.M. 1981.
The Dialogic magination: Four Essays. (M. Holquist, Ed.; C. Emerson and M. Holquist, Trans.)
Austin: University of Texas Press.

Ballard, J.G. 2007.
"The Larval State of a New Kind of Architecture."
The Guardian, October 7, 2007.
www.guardian.co.uk/artanddesign/2007/oct/08/architecture.bilbao

Barthes, Roland. 1972.
Mythologies.
New York: Hill & Wang.

Barthes, Roland. 1979.
Trans. Richard Howard.
The Eiffel Tower and Other Mythologies (Richard Howard, Trans).
New York: Hill & Wang.

Barthes. Roland. 1982.
Empire of Signs.
New York: Hill & Wang.

Baudrillard, Jean. 1996.
"Disneyworld Company" (Francois Debrix, Trans.).
Liberation, March 4, 1996.

Baudrillard, Jean. 1998.
The Consumer Society: Myths and Structures.
Thousand Oaks, CA: Sage.

Berger, Arthur Asa. 2004.
Deconstructing Travel: Cultural Perspectives on Tourism.
Walnut Creek, CA: AltaMira Press.

Berger, Arthur Asa. 2010.
Tourism in Japan: An Ethno-Semiotic Analysis.
Bristol, UK: Channel View.

Benjamin, Walter.
"The Work of Art in the Age of Mechanical Reproduction."
In Gerald Mast, and Marshall Cohen (Eds.), *Film Theory and Criticism: Introductory Readings.* 1974.
New York: Oxford University Press.

References

Benjamin, Walter. 1999.
The Arcades Project.
Cambridge, MA: The Belknap Press of Harvard University Press.

Boorstin, Daniel. 1961.
The Image: A Guide to Pseudo-Events in America.
New York: Harper and Row.

Brody, Michael. 1976.
"The Wonderful World of Disney: Its Psychological Appeal."
American Imago 33: 350–360.

Byne, Rory.
"Tourism Threatens Historic City Known as 'Soul' of Laos."
www.lonelyplanet.com/thorntree/thread.jspa?threadID=1742726

Castaneda, Quatzil E.
"Tourism Wars in the Yucatan."
American Anthropological Association.
www.aaanet.org/press/an/infocus/Heritage_In_Focus/Castaneda.htm

Cohen, Erik.
In Kotler et al. *Marketing for Hospitality and Tourism,* Second Edition. 1999.
Upper Saddle River: Prentice Hall

Cohen, Erik. 2008.
"The Changing Faces of Contemporary Tourism."
Society 5 (4): 330–333.

Cohen, Shaye D. 2010
The Significance of Yavneh and Other Essays on Jewish Hellenism.
Tubingen, Germany: Mohr Siebeck .

de Saussure, Ferdinand. 1915/1916.
Trans. W. Baskin
Course in General Linguistics (W. Baskin, Trans.).
New York: McGraw-Hill.

Dearborn, Lynne M , and John C. Stallmeyer. 2010.
Inconvenient Heritage: Erasure and Global Tourism in Luang Prabang.
Walnut Creek, CA· Left Coast Press, Inc.

Dubech and d'Espezel, *Histoire de Paris.*
In W. Benjamin, *The ArcadesProject.* 1999.
Cambridge, MA· Belknap Press of Harvard University Press.

Eliade, Mircea. 1961.
The Sacred and the Profane: The Nature of Religion.
New York: Harper & Row.

eprints.lse.ac.uk/3624/1/Bilbao_city_report_(final).pdf

Fallow, Deborah.
pewresearch.org/pubs/776/china-internet

Fairchild, Henry Pratt. 1967.
Dictionary of Sociology and Related Sciences.
New York: Littlefield, Adams & Company.

Figes, Orlando. 2002.
Natasha's Dance: A Cultural History of Russia.
New York: Metropolitan Books.

Fjellman, S.M. 1992.
Vinyl Leaves: Walt Disney World and America.
Boulder, CO: Westview Press.

Freud, S. 1963
In Rieff, P. (Ed.) *Freud: Character and Culture.*
New York: Collier Books.

Freud, Sigmund. 1953.
A General Introduction to Psychoanalysis.
New York: Permabooks.

Geertz, Clifford. 1973.
The Interpretation of Cultures: Selected Essays.
New York: Basic Books.

Glaser,Stephanie A.
"The Eiffel Tower: Cultural Icon, Cultural Interface."
In K. G. Tomaselli and David Scott (Eds.) *Cultural Icons.* 2009.
Walnut Creek, CA: Left Coast Press, Inc..

Gottdiener, Mark. 1982.
"Disneyland: a Utopian Urban Space."
Journal of Contemporary Ethnography 11 (2):139–162.

Gottdiener, Mark. 1996.
The Theming of America: Dreams, Visions and Commercial Space.
Boulder, CO: Westview Press.

Hall, Peter.
Review of James Holston's *The Modernist City: An Anthropological Critique of Brasilia*
in the *Los Angeles Times.* March 4, 1990.
articles.latimes.com/1990-03-04/books/bk-2454_1_james-holston

Haskell, Francis, quoted in Watkin, D. (2001)
Morality and Architecture; Revisited.
Chicago: University of Chicago Press.

Holquist, Michael (Ed.) 1981.
The Dialogic Imagination: Four Essays by M.M. Bakhtin.
Austin: University of Texas Press.

Huyssen, Andreas. 1986.
After the Great Divide: Modernism, Mass Culture, Postmodernism.
Bloomington: Indiana University Press.

Ishizawa, Yoshiaki. 2008.
Along the Royal Road to Angkor.
New York: Weathhill.

Jemsel, Samuel.
In Elkan Nathan Adler.
Jewish Travelers. 1930.
London: Routledge.

Jencks, Charles.
"Postmodern vs. Late Modern"
In *Ingeborg Hoesterey (Ed.), Zeitgeist in Babel: The Postmodernist Controversy.* 1991.
Bloomington: Indiana University Press.

Jewish Virtual Library.
www.jewishvirtuallibrary.org/jsource/Judaism/masada.html

Jordan, David.
www.davidjayjordan.com/SonicStoneLevitation.html

References

Kotler, Philip, John Bowen, and James Makens. 1999.
Marketing for Hospitality and Tourism. Second Edition.
Upper Saddle River, NJ: Prentice Hall.

Lakoff, George, and Mark Johnson. 1980.
Metaphors We Live By.
Chicago: University of Chicago Press.

Lonely Planet India. 2005.
Locked Bag 1, Footscray, Victoria 1.

Lyotard, Jean-François. 1984.
The Postmodern Condition: A Report on Knowledge (G. Bennington and B. Massumi, Trans.).
Minneapolis: University of Minnesota Press.

MacCannell, Dean. 1976.
The Tourist: A New Theory of the Leisure Class.
New York: Schocken Books.

Magnoni, Aline, Traci Ardren, and Scott Hutson.
"Tourism in the Mundo Maya: Inventions and (Mis)Representations of Maya Identity."
Archaeologies: Journal of the World Archaeological Congress (2007) Vol. 3, No. 3, December 2007:
353–383.

Milgram, Stanley. 1976. "
The Image Freezing Machine."
Society: November/December: 7–12.

Morris, Jan. 1982.
Destinations: Essays from Rolling Stone.
New York: Oxford University Press.

Morris, Jan. 1984.
Journeys.
New York: Oxford University Press.

Mosher, Gouverneur. 1980.
Kyoto: A Comparative Guide.
Rutland, VT: Charles E. Tuttle.

National Geographic.
science.nationalgeographic.com/science/archaeology/giza-pyramids/

O'Barr, William O. 1994.
Culture and the Ad: Exploring Otherness in the World.
Boulder, Co: Westview Press.

Ontero, Maria
www.humanrights.gov/2012/01/24/statement-by-the-special-coordinator-for-tibetan-issues-maria-otero/

Osborne, P. 2000.
www.lancs.ac.uk/fass/sociology/papers/urry-globalising-the-tourist-gaze.pdf

Patai, Raphael. 1972.
Myth and Modern Man.
Englewood Cliffs, NJ: Prentice Hall.

Peirce, C.S.
In J. J. Zeyman, "Peirce's Theory of Signs." In T. A. Sebeok (Ed.) *A Perfusion of Signs.* 1977.
Bloomington: Indiana University Press.

Picard, Michel. 1996.
Bali Cultural Tourism and Touristic Culture.
Singapore: Archipelago Press.

Picard, Michel. 1999.
"Creating a New Version of Paradise" in Eric Oey (Ed.),
Bali, Indonesia.
Singapore: Periplus Adventure Guides.

Plog, Stanley. 1974.
"Why Destinations Rise and Fall in Popularity."
Cornell Hotel and Restaurant Administration Quarterly.
Vol. 14, No. 4: 55–58.

Powers, John. 2007
Introduction to Tibetan Buddhism.
Ithaca, NY: Snow Lion.

Rieff, Philip (Ed.) 1963.
Freud: Character and Culture.
New York: Collier Books.

Rolef, Susan Hattis.
"On the Masada Complex."
www.jewishvirtuallibrary.org/jsource/Judaism/masada.html

Romer, John. 2007
The Great Pyramid: Ancient Egypt Revisited.
Cambridge, England: Cambridge University Press.

Schickel, Richard. 1968.
The Disney Version.
New York: Avon Books.

Smith, Hedrick. 1976.
The Russians.
New York: Quadrangle Books.

Sofield, Trevor, and Sarah Li.
"Tourism Development and Cultural Policies in China."
Annals of Tourism. Vol. 25, No. 2:362–392.

Solomon, Jack. 1990.
The Signs of Our Time: The Secret Meanings of Everyday Life.
New York: Harper & Row.

Thompson, M., R. Ellis, and A. Wildavsky. 1990.
Cultural Theory.
Boulder, CO: Westview.

Treib, Mark, and Ron Herman. 1993. *A
Guide to the Gardens of Kyoto.*
Tokyo: Shufunotomo.

Tucker, Hazel. 1997.
"The Ideal Village: Interactions Through Tourism in Central Anatolia."
In Simone Abram, Jacqueline Waldren, and Donald V. I. McLeod (Eds.),
Tourists and Tourism: Identifying with People and Places. Oxford, England: Berg.

Tyrnauer, Matt.
"Architecture in the Age of Frank Gehry."
Vanity Fair. August, 2010.
www.vanityfair.com/culture/features/2010/08/architecture-survey-201008

UNESCO website.
whc.unesco.org/en/list/668

References

UNWTO World Tourism Barometer.
www.unwto.org/facts/eng/barometer.htm

Urry, John. 2001.
"Globalizing the Tourist Gaze."
Published by the Department of Sociology, Lancaster University.
www.barcelonametropolis.cat/en/page.asp?id=23&ui=12

Venuri, Robert, Denise Scott Brown, and Steven Izenour. 1977.
Learning from Las Vegas: The Forgotten Symbolism or Architectural Form.
Cambridge, MA: MIT Press.

Wang, Ning. 2000.
Tourism and Modernity: A Sociological Analysis.
Oxford, England: Pergamon.

Warner, Langdon. 1952.
The Enduring Art of Japan.
Cambridge, MA: Harvard University Press.

Watkin, D. 2001.
Morality and Architecture; Revisited
Chicago: University of Chicago Press

Wellman, Don.
"The Birth of Modernism."
faculty.dwc.edu/wellman/Birth_Modernism.html

Wildavsky, Aaron B.
"Choosing Preferences by Constructing Institutions: A Cultural Theory of Preference Formation." In Arthur Asa Berger (Ed.), *Political Culture and Public Opinion.* 1989.
New Brunswick, NJ: Transaction Books.

Wolfe, Tom. 1965.
The Kandy-Kolored Tangerine-Flake Streamline Baby.
New York: Farrar, Strauss and Giroux.

Woolf, Virginia "Mr. Bennett and Mrs. Brown."
www.columbia.edu/~em36/MrBennettAndMrsBrown.pdf

Yamasa Institute.
www.yamasa.org/index.html

Yamashita, Shinji.
Review of Michel Picard, *Bali: Cultural Tourism and Touristic Culture.*
In *Indonesia.* No. 67. April 1999:177–182.
Southeast Asia Program Publications at Cornell University.

Yamashita, Shinji. 2003.
Bali and Beyond: Explorations in the Anthropology of Tourism.
New York: Berghahn Books.

Zeyman, Jay. J.
"Peirce's Theory of Signs."
In T. S. Sebeok (Ed.), *A Perfusion of Signs.* 1977.
Bloomington: Indiana University Press.

Zukin, Sharon. 2005.
Point of Purchase: How Shopping Changed American Culture.
New York: Routledge.

About the Author

Arthur Asa Berger is professor emeritus of Broadcast and Electronic Communication Arts at San Francisco State University, where he taught between 1965 and 2003. He has been a visiting professor in Italy, Germany, Hong Kong, and China and has lectured in more than a dozen countries. He lectured in Italy as a Fulbright scholar in 1963 and in Argentina as a Fulbright Senior Specialist in 2012. Berger is author of over one hundred articles and has authored or edited more than seventy-five books on media, popular culture, social theory, humor, and tourism. His books have been translated into nine languages. Among his recent books are *Seeing is Believing: An Introduction to Visual Communication; What Objects Mean: An Introduction to Material Culture; The Objects of Affection; Media and Society; Media and Communication Research Methods; Bloom's Morning; Ads, Fads and Consumer Culture; Understanding American Icons;* and *Shop 'Til You Drop.* He was elected to the University of Iowa School of Journalism and Mass Communication's "Hall of Fame" in 2009.